Writing on Water

Judit Niran Frigyesi

Writing on Water
The Sounds of Jewish Prayer

Budapest–New York

Published in Hungarian in 2014 as *Jelek a vízen* by Libri Kiadó

Published in 2018 by
Central European University Press

Nádor utca 11, H-1051 Budapest, Hungary
Tel: +36-1-327-3138 or 327-3000
Fax: +36-1-327-3183
E-mail: ceupress@press.ceu.edu
Website: www.ceupress.com
224 West 57th Street, New York NY 10019, USA

Library of Congress Cataloging-in-Publication Data

Names: Niran Frigyesi, Judit, author.
Title: Writing on water : the sounds of Jewish prayer / Judit Niran Frigyesi.
Other titles: Jelek a vízen. English | The Sounds of Jewish prayer
Description: New York : Central European University Press, [2018]
Identifiers: LCCN 2017048944 | ISBN 9789633862575 (pbk.)
Subjects: LCSH: Jews—Europe, Central—Interviews. | Oral tradition—Europe, Central. | Orthodox Judaism—Europe, Central—History—20th century. | Judaism—Europe, Central—Customs and practices. | Judaism—Sudy and teaching—Europe, Central. | Jews—Europe, Central—Music. | Music—Performance—Europe, Central—20th century. | Holocaust, Jewish (1939-1945)—Europe, Central. | Communism—Europe, Central—History—20th century.
Classification: LCC DS135.E83 F7413 2018 | DDC 296.4/509439—dc23 LC record available at https://lccn.loc.gov/20170489440

Preface

This book is an attempt to grasp the meaning of *sound in prayer*. I became first aware of the tremendous importance of sound in prayer, and possibly in all human spiritual expression, during my research among traditional Jewish communities of Eastern Europe. *The Sounds of Jewish Prayer* in the subtitle of this book refers to the sounds of these communities. For these traditional Jews, it was an unspoken axiom that the essence of existence (of God) cannot be grasped by words and logic but only by the heart. These people lived by a philosophy of the heart.

Philosophy is the study or contemplation of the fundamental nature of reality and existence. The word φιλοσοφία means "love of wisdom" or "friend of wisdom"—perhaps there was an emotional element embedded in the name at the birth of the discipline. In the course of the centuries, however, philosophy—at least Western philosophy—developed its method by using a systematic approach, rational language, argumentation and logic.

But what happens when we realize that logic, rationality and words do not lead us to the understanding of the fundamental nature of existence? What happens when we realize that the human mind is unable to grasp, through logic and arguments, the essential nature of concepts such as eternity, infinity, nothingness, soul and death? Eternity and death cannot be understood; they can only be felt (or thought to be felt) through sensations. But we do have sensations—even a child can experience the fear of death.

In the culture of traditional Jews in Eastern Europe, words and arguments had enormous prestige. Yet at the same time, there was the tacit understanding that the essence of existential phenomena lies beyond words. And more: if the believer is not capable of transcending the rational and logical meaning of words, then words become a barrier to the higher reality that he or she is trying to reach.

It appears to be the consensus in many cultures that in order to grasp the existential phenomena our sensations hint at, one needs to arrive at a transcendental state. Transcendental states can be achieved by a variety of techniques and take on the most diverse forms within religious rituals. East European Jews had their own unique ways.

Could the anthropologist, who, as it often happens, becomes "half-native," convey anything of this experience? Should she translate an experience impossible to verbalize and systematize into the language of systems, logic and words? Most scholars would answer this question in the affirmative. Yet many of us suffer from the demand of scholarship to clarify what is not possible to clarify and to systematize what is not possible to systematize. I collapsed under the weight of this demand. I began to feel that by sticking to the rules of scholarly writing, I betrayed the people who entrusted me with their music, culture, thoughts and philosophy. My scholarly writing failed to transmit what was most important to the practitioners of these rituals: *the poetics* in *the sound* of prayer.

The French philosopher Gaston Bachelard opens his work *The Poetics of Space* with the following lines: "A philosopher who has evolved his entire thinking from the fundamental themes of the philosophy of science, and followed the main line of the [...] growing rationalism of contemporary science as closely as he could, must forget his learning and break with all his habits of philosophical research, if he wants to study the problems posed by the poetic imagination. For here [...] the long day-in, day-out effort of putting together and constructing his thoughts is ineffectual. One must be receptive, receptive to the image at the moment it appears: if there be a philosophy of poetry, it must appear and reappear through a significant verse, in total adherence to an isolated image; to be exact, in the very ecstasy of the newness of the image [...] [The poetic image] emerges into the consciousness as a direct product of the heart, soul and being of man, apprehended in his actuality."

I was dealing with the poetic imagination. It was the poetic imagination that created the terrain and the paths that led towards grasping existential problems. I experienced atmospheres, colors, sounds, and melodies, and in spite of the fact that this was not poetry in the narrow sense of the word, these *were* "poetic images." The sounds of the ritual affected only those who were receptive "in total adherence to an isolated image (sound) [...] in the very ecstasy of the image (sound)," in the moment of their emergence "into the consciousness as a direct product of the heart, soul and being of man, apprehended in his actuality."

At some point during my research, poetic fragments began to infiltrate my writing, parallel to or sometimes replacing the scholarly formulations of my subject. Simple factual details of my observations took on metaphorical meaning. My writing gradually became a journey toward a poetic language that echoed and emulated the spiritual poetic sound-milieu it attempted to describe.

The spirituality of the sound I lived through in the Jewish prayer compelled me to move beyond it. Over the years, my research has become the search for an understanding of *an essence in sound* and *an essence in prayer*. What matters to me is not the specific functions of elements within the framework of formal religion, but a fundamental human experience: the soul's journey toward the sensation of what is incomprehensible and inexpressible in our existence.

Of course, it is impossible to compose an entire book merely of poetic images, and there are numerous sections of straightforward, sometimes even humorous prose that recount events. But mainly, this text is a series of prose poems, and the images are metaphors for the music through which I descended to the depths of prayer. The tone of poetic imagery is set already with the motto ("… The taste of river. Behind the wall an old man prays …") and by the first scene: "'You have not seen anything yet. Come tomorrow at a quarter to seven.' I prepare my coffee in the dark. My parents and brother are asleep. The street's morning tumult is muted by the wall of water around my senses, as if what I was about to hear were already protecting me."

The reader will discover multiple meanings and themes in these sentences, which reoccur throughout the book. The "wall," the prayer from "behind the wall" (or "behind the curtain"), dawn and darkness, the enigmatic invitation for an early morning gathering, the sense of an invisible protective padding, water and the "wall of water"—these are metaphors for the soundscapes and atmospheres of the prayer houses. These soundscapes penetrated all corners of everyday life, theirs and mine, and it was precisely this penetration that gave them meaning.

I am embarrassed and reluctant to write what I have just written, because the images were not constructed logically, nor were their metaphorical meanings planned, and I feel that it may be wrong to explain them the way I have done above. I often only realized such meanings after my readers noticed them: the above analysis is from one of my reviewers, to whom I am indebted for her observations. At the time of writing I did not think of metaphors and connections. I wrote the first version of this text in a trance, while colors vibrated around me, and the space of the synagogues resounded in my head. I was inside an atmosphere, as I was during those years when I carried out the core of this research.

Everything in this book happened—nothing has been invented for the sake of poetry. Apart from skipping a few details, I have altered nothing in the course of the events. Similarly, the photographs were taken at the places I describe in the book. All the characters are real and most of the texts I attribute to them are transcriptions, sometimes word for word, in translation, from the tapes I recorded. The poetic aspect concerns the form and the style, not the content.

It is possible to read this book only for the information it contains. But readers interested only in facts and technical analyses will find much of the text to be fanciful digressions from the subject. Many parts were sketched originally as poems or as poetic prose. I hope I have succeeded in molding these fragments into a story, but the end result is still, and is intentionally, like a succession of short stories. They could be read in themselves, and perhaps even out of order.

I would like to ask the reader to suspend the expectations one has when dealing with a scholarly text, and read this book as if it were poetry—poetry that transmits knowledge. I ask this because, paraphrasing Bachelard, the day-in, day-out effort of constructing a logical system proved to be ineffectual for the author of this book. In dealing with the subject of her study, she could not but follow the call of the imagination, reliving the ecstasy of a new poetic image in each sound.

I thank you for opening this book and hope that you will enjoy what it tells you.

Judit Niran Frigyesi

I. The Sound of a Thousand Walls

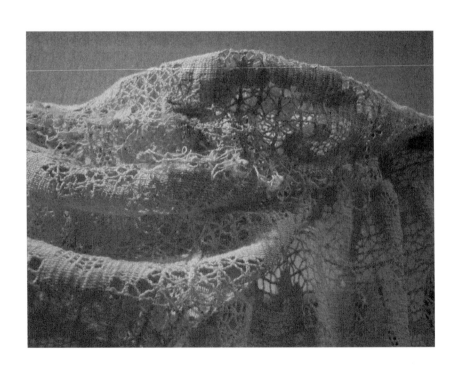

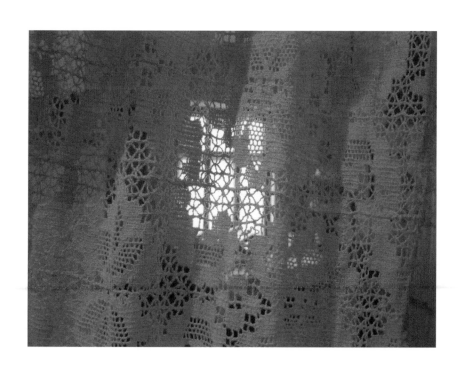

The Taste of River

… The taste of river. Behind the wall an old man prays …

"You have not seen anything yet. Come tomorrow at a quarter to seven." I prepare my coffee in the dark. My parents and brother are asleep. The street's morning tumult is muted by the wall of water around my senses, as if what I was about to hear were already protecting me.

I walk across the park. Emmanuel is already at the gate. He nods and, without a word, slips through the bolted gateway, a colossal tunnel, like those built for the old village houses to allow carriages through. I notice a stairway. Emmanuel keeps going, through the tunnel, out into the snow-glittered courtyard. We cross the courtyard and at its far end arrive at another bolted gateway. A narrow stairwell that smells of damp plaster leads up to the room on the second floor, where they are expecting us. We enter, silently, through the open door.

The room is small, just big enough for those who gathered here this morning. Emmanuel goes to the front and joins a group of men discussing something in front of the windows in which hang delicate lace curtains. They are dressed in simple clothes in shades of brown and grey—warm and restrained colors, like the sound of their muted voices.

There are several such groups scattered in the room. The buzz of their conversation is accompanied by calm but animated gestures that bespeak a sense of security. Others stand around fumbling with this or that—taking off winter coats, unfolding their prayer shawls, unpacking prayer books from multiple layers of newspaper. A few older men, already in their seats, stare idly in the air, perhaps still dreaming dawn's lingering dream, and from the depths of the room someone is already whispering his prayer. Gradually, plodding their way through the row of benches, each man finds his place. Those who had not yet done so now put on their *tfilin* and wrap their heads and shoulders in the *talis*. The subdued colors of the morning become animated with the gliding, flowing waves of black spirals and blue-white sails.

I remain standing by the door. Suddenly, one of them notices the unfamiliar face. He goes to the back row, picks up a book and begins to walk toward me. I feel weak, unsure about what will happen next. With an expression that is impossible to read, he puts the prayer book in front of me and draws a white lace curtain between my bench and the rest of the room.

Budapest, 1976. I take my place of sacred isolation, the only woman and the only non-believer in the empty women's section of a secret Jewish prayer house. Soon, prayer will descend on me through the arabesque of white lace. And so I will remain: close to them, flying with the gestures of their souls, while tied to the earth by the loneliness of my alien existence.

It begins slowly, almost unnoticeably. Speaking dissolves into a melodious noise and, like flecks of shimmer from the end of the world congeal in beams, the scattered words melt into chanting.

I observe them as though this were a film. The morning prayer is like a flight of birds. Little muted cries fly off their lips and whirl about in all directions, and the singsong fragments braid themselves into solid vibration. I listen to the sounds as if they were music and as if music were a peregrination, a fairytale, a caressing hand, glitter and gleam of a trickling stream—ancient, transparent and legendary.

Suddenly, a chill runs down my spine. It is as if a door, behind which a memory previously unknown and unrecognized lay hidden, had been flung open, their prayer and me—I, here, among them. As if all this were happening to someone else, as if it had already happened before within the shrieks and rattling of a languishing dream...

a tree branch breaks and in the rift
of the glow of golden blue sounds

the deep anguish beneath the waters
flings itself off the trash heap of days

among pale faces of dreams beyond dreams
the wing of memory takes my hand

there is no trial and no deliverance,
it was me, in a life before my birth

spring of sounds from which they drink
waves which engulf without will

silver rain falls from an unknown source
and rivers spill over beyond their time

It is not true that witnessing the life of others makes you more experienced. When you peek through the keyhole, catching a glance that betrays a faith you do not share, all that remains is confusion of the heart. Placing your body next to theirs does not mean that you are with them. You have to open the wounds and slip inside through the torn surface of your life. You must gulp down your sorrows and your nights, until your eyes open to see them.

(I am a child alone at night, helpless. In the dark, father runs to my bed and caresses my cheeks. I cannot stop screaming. He takes me into his arms and holds me until my heartbeat slows down and my feet turn cold. He pulls the blanket over my body, talking all the time. *Don't be afraid, you're young, only a child, with a whole life to live*. My heart sinks. Time has nothing to do with it. The fear of death in a child is not the fear of impending death. It is the fear of *death*. The fear of the hand, the horror of nothing. It is the child's awakening into existence.

Death was around me, in every corner. My mother and father did not talk about the dead bodies lying around in our house. The dead themselves had to speak. But they were unknown to me, like my own dreams. My parents were also unknown to me. Their profession and their secular existence were the glass wall separating them from atavistic beliefs, and the family was the womb into which they climbed for shelter from their unspeakable memories. In the rush of days, they forgot to speak. They forgot to say that nothing releases those born with a fear of death.)

On that morning in the prayer room, I stood voiceless and stunned like a child who dreamt the forbidden dream. I was mesmerized, and for reasons that were incomprehensible to me, ashamed. When the mourner's *Kaddish* began, I sneaked out of the prayer room. I could not face them. Out on the street, I began to walk and soon got lost in the unfamiliar district. Finally, I found the boulevard and got on the tram. I held the handrail and stared at the speedy flight of decorated palaces. The streets reflected the colors of an ordinary winter morning, as though nothing had happened. Instead of going to class, I went home.

Rolled up in the corner of the sofa that also served as my bed, I gazed out the window at the crumbling plaster of the neighboring house, and above it, the grey sky. I sat for a long time, my mind dulled. Then I took out the family photo album and began leafing through it: my parents, grandparents, great-grandparents, great-uncles and aunts, their uncles and aunts and cousins, and more relatives, obscure relationships, lives and fates. The more elusive the traces of connecting reality became in the maze of uncharted glances, the more I realized, bemused and dazed, that they all looked alike, and reminded me dimly of a port from which I had set sail before consciousness took hold of me.

I needed a few days to come to my senses. Even with a calm mind, I had to admit that I had never heard a sound more mysterious—and yet casual—than the sound of that prayer house. I had never imagined that music could be so perfect and spiritual and still so intimate and unpretentious. No, it was not music. It was an *atmosphere*: whirlwind, draught and breath—mythical and enigmatic, solemn and secure like a mountain range.

In the course of the following years I often returned to that prayer house. It became a routine: I enter the room, take off my coat, unpack my prayer book and exchange a smile with the men, who gradually got used to my face. I draw the curtain and open the book. As long as I bathe in the radiance of the sound of their prayer, I feel no weight and no sorrow. I stand still until the last *Kaddish* fades, pull back the curtain, wish them a good day and leave. I get on the tram, hold on to the handrail and look out at the palaces lining the boulevard. The streets reflect the colors of an ordinary morning and I feel nothing. Being with them and listening to their sounds, it is easy to go beyond and easy to come back.

After some weeks, one of the men asked me for my Jewish name. I told him. From then on, my name was included in the blessing after the Torah reading on Shabes. But I did not ask for their names and did not get familiar with them. I sheltered these mornings like one shelters a dream, so that life's everydays would not etch their scores on its surface—so that it remain like the first morning: a mirage emanating from the soul's labyrinth.

The Silence of Unsung Songs

Father's photo albums are chronological. Their orderliness is the unconditional surrender after the eternally lost battle with the ghoulish pathos of remembrance of unnamable things. My father opened a new chapter when my mother came into his life, a year before I was born. The albums that date from after these memorable events contain dozens of pictures of my mother and a richly documented account of my development and—starting two years later, when he was born—of my brother's as well. There are a few photos of my father, like the one in which he is seen holding his head against mine,

and occasionally the four of us appear together: at the Margaret Bridge after our Sunday ice-cream walk, or huddled together, apprehensive of the invading waves, at the edge of a bench during a boat trip on Lake Balaton. But the theme is mostly my mother and the children: my mother looking inside the baby carriage, my mother on the telephone, with a toy bear, in army uniform, and in her white doctor's gown with the stethoscope around her neck; my brother and I in the play pen, in the park, by the Danube, at the Santa Claus celebration at school; my brother balancing on the swing; and my tiny tulle-dressed body on an enormous stage, arms outstretched and mouth open, dancing my solo at the ballet gala. And there is the picture taken by Aunt Cser in her studio: the whole family together—those who survived, that is—sitting close to one another while a light beam from an unknown source streams over us, fleeing the picture in the bottom right corner.

My ancestors are arranged in separate albums. Wrinkleless alabaster faces frozen in reverie before the mysteriously waving curtains of the studio are mingled with smiles and grimaces captured in the miniature copies of overexposed amateur photographs. My father recorded the time and place with neat handwriting on the back of each photograph. He listed everyone by their full name—even his parents, his children and himself. This meant that in the case of the women, there were at least two and often three full names: a maiden name and a married name, and for those who had married more than once, several married names. As if he was preparing the album for a stranger to whom he would one day have to prove that it did not contain anything illegal, that no data were hidden, and that the whole undertaking was innocent, insignificant for the world at large.

But the photographs were not innocent. There was, for instance, the picture of his parents from Luhačovice, taken in 1934, during their last vacation before the inferno. On the photo, my grandfather looks somewhat overweight and my grandmother is so chubby in her bright flower dress that she looks several years older than her age. Round and heavy, they walk toward the photographer energetically; their mouths are full of laughter. On another photograph, from 1943, they pose for the camera in a studio. My grandmother is wearing a simple black dress, ornamented only by a thin white collar; my grandfather, in suit and necktie, looks official and apprehensive. Their lips are pressed together, and although they look into the camera, I cannot catch their eyes— nor can I comprehend what it is about this picture that evokes in me a feeling of infinite sorrow. On the last picture, they are standing in front of an apartment building. From the way grandfather is turned, it seems that he is holding her hand. The photograph was taken in 1953, nine years after the Nazi occupation, five years into Rákosi's communist regime, in the year of Stalin's death and a year before his own.

It is hard to explain why, already as a child, this last photograph moved me so deeply. It was perhaps the sense of withdrawal. My grandmother looks into the camera as if by chance. My grandfather, turned slightly towards her, gazes out of the picture as though he had noticed something troublesome in the distance. My grandmother's face: "Photograph us? Why? What's the point?" My grandfather's face: "I see something over there— but don't worry, things will get better."

But I realize now that it was not so much their expressions but the familiarity of their faces that crushed me. This is how grown-ups looked, I thought, and in the case of my grandmother it was not hard for me to recognize the person I knew. The Luhačovice photograph, however, was alien. It reminded me of nothing. I could not imagine that such a fat and happy couple had any relation to me.

Crawled into my father's lap, I kept turning the pages. When we reached this photograph, I grabbed him firmly so I would not fall as we plunged into the depths, leaving behind a fairyland, sinking millions of years from the Luhačovice photograph to those taken after the 1940s. Never again, I thought. Never again will children have grandparents strolling along a path bursting with laughter.

I loved this last photograph, because the expression on my grandmother's face reminded me of how she looked when she told me something I have never forgotten. My parents were at work and she was looking after us. We were playing tag and my brother ran into her. She fell. She was not exactly stable anyway, and walked with a cane. Unable to get up, she remained where she was and her tears began to flow. Not knowing what to do, I kneeled down next to her. She sobbed a bit, then calmed herself, and, still on the ground, she began to talk to me: "I hope they don't get any worse, my legs. I have to be able to walk. Soon I will have to walk you to the music school. It's far, you can't go alone, and your parents have no time. But you have to go. Your father isn't sure about it. But I know that when you grow up, you will do something with music."

The world of my mother as I remember it from childhood: her care for patients, love for her mother, and with the little breath that was left in her in the evenings, love for her family. And fear. She wore fear like a coat of armor—fear of the new regulations at the hospital, fear of the border guard, fear that we would get lost during an excursion, fear that my brother would be late for school, and most of all, fear of hurting someone, God forbid. Thick, impenetrable walls of fear protected the inside of her soul, her refuge of sanity safely preserved against the world's insanity. Like the enchanted princess in the fairytale, she was happy within the walnut's shell. Only there, deep inside, did she dare be inventive, joyful and artistic.

(These days, when I am almost as old as she was when she became a grandmother, we often go out to a café together, just the two of us. Padded in noise, she sheds the walnut's shell from her skin. Her face shines, and I notice that I am talking to her as to a friend my age.)

The world of my father as I remember it from childhood: his eyes fixed on the ground, focusing only on those things that fell within the meter wide radius around him. His father, also a doctor, died before I was born, and his mother died when I was six. True, a few others survived from among his family and friends before the war. But most of them became an item on the list of names he sent to Yad Vashem.

With my father, everything is either too close or too far. The way you cut the cheese is important. It is important because if you cut it the wrong way, you will not be able to fit the leftover cheese in the right way in the right container. There is a right way for everything. But life stories are boring. They are all the same. No need to talk too much.

In my childhood memories, I can never recall his face. I know how he looked from the photographs, but I do not remember it. I remember the touch of his hand on my forehead when I was sick. I remember the caressing warmth during terrifying nights— his body around mine as he held me tightly so that I would not fall out of the world. Only he knows the secret of wordless caring that expects no gratitude.

There goes a man. He has a wife and two children. They are everything. The rest is betrayal. Distrust any society larger than four people.

My father cannot sing. He is incapable of producing any sound that resembles singing, and when he tries, we have to laugh.

My maternal grandmother, however, would sing to me and I loved it when she sang. I, too, could sing, and she was proud of me. "When you were little, you knew so many songs. When my friends from the laboratory came to see us, we made you stand on the table. You sang a song, we clapped and one of us would lift you to take you down. But before your feet reached the ground, you would cry out and ask to sing more. Then the same thing happened. You never wanted to stop."

I remember vaguely, as in a dream, flying up to a table in a stranger's strong arms, then back to the floor, and then back up again. I remember neither the songs, nor the taste of singing.

The scattered pieces of my childhood memory do not cohere. They are like plates of rock smashed against each other in an earthquake; and for the geologist, each plate holds a story of millions of years of adventures. And still, when the isolated fragments of this unexplored, impaired and vestigial childhood gush to the surface in myriad incarnations, they embrace my present with full and radiating perspective. As if the past were like a monumental painting of a landscape, which the painter, after filling it with minia-

ture figures crammed to the point of incomprehensibility, in one melancholic moment, washed over with the color of faint brown.

I lived under the protective veil of gentle silence. In my family, the most important things were never said. One does not need to speak too much about oneself—not to anyone, surely not to people outside of the family, and absolutely not to the world at large. One does not need to tell *the story*, because we know it anyway and *the others* would not understand.

I watched their hesitations and intimations; I collected the shards of their life stations like pieces of a broken mirror, hoping to assemble the chronicle. There were no objects in our house and no events in our lives that one would have recognized as Jewish. Signs of the Jewish religion did not belong to the landscape of Communist Budapest. The crumbling dark walls of abandoned synagogues blended in with the city's omnipresent decay, and the small communities of practicing Jews made sure to remain invisible.

I have no memories of ever having had a conversation about (our) Jewishness. That we were Jewish was so obvious, so much an ordinary matter of everyday existence, that it did not even occur to me to ask what Jewishness really meant. Those things, which I now realize were mildly dangerous at the time, like receiving recordings and picture books from my Israeli uncle and having stacks of Hebrew language conversation books, were routine aspects of my life, like my two long braids of brownish-blond hair. The smiles of the young girls in the *kibbutzim* in the 1950s-style drawing in my Israeli children's book were as basic to my early visual experiences as the very similarly looking Hungarian peasant girls who smiled at me from the pages of my first year elementary school book.

Once my father told me that I should not ask my step-grandfather about that pretty girl whose photo was on his dresser, and in general should not ask about *those things*. That little girl was Ancika, my step-grandfather's daughter whom he lost together with his wife in the flames of Auschwitz, or, as we used to say, who "did not come back." "Yes, another one of those," I thought and made sure my glance would not fall on that picture when my step-grandfather was around. He had lost his wife and daughter and my maternal grandmother had lost her husband, so it was natural for them to get married after the war. They had a good life together.

"Yes, another one. Like my grandfather." I did not know exactly how my maternal grandfather died, and of course, it never crossed my mind to ask. In our circles, the sentence "did not come back" was a euphemism for any one of the thousand forms of death connected with the mysterious name "Auschwitz." Whenever I heard of someone who "did not come back," I felt (though perhaps would not have said it with so many words): "Yes, of course. Jews are always on the road. They are always going somewhere. Some come back, some don't. That we are alive is an accident and that I was born at all is also an accident."

I missed my grandfather terribly, even though I never met him and no one ever spoke of him. I longed for him the way one longs for the mythical past. You long, senselessly and with a mad force of will, to reverse the unfathomable loss of something you have never known. Sometime before I entered school, I stopped singing. The last song remained stuck in my throat.

I was already in high school when my step-grandfather died. I was with my grandmother when she unpacked her husband's drawer. She took out the neatly folded shirts one by one and placed them on the table. Suddenly, a set of old prayer books surfaced. My step-grandfather's first wife and daughter had left theirs behind when they were forced out onto the road. I opened the smallest one and read the inscription: "To my dear Ancika, in the month of February 1944, from your loving father." My grandmother dug deeper into the drawer and pulled out an embroidered *talis* holder and boxes of *tfilin*. After the war in Budapest, only the most religious Jews put on *tfilin*. "I had no idea," she said, her face pale.

My heart sank. Did he actually pray, in secret, with a prayer shawl and phylacteries? I was unable to comfort my grandmother. Tears rolled down my cheeks for her husband, whom I could never really love while he was alive. I watched my grandmother staring at the *tfilin* with a motionless face, her back straight, and her hands limp on the table like question marks. My step-grandfather died of a heart attack while giving a speech at a Party meeting.

One day, many years after my paternal grandmother died, my father took me to see the house where they had lived when he was a child. I remembered the house. On weekends grandmother came to stay with us, but we also visited her a few times in her small house, in what seemed to me a faraway, exotic place—the workers' district where my grandfather had been the neighborhood family doctor before the war. My father showed me around. He talked about the people and the neighborhood in the days when he was a child, and described the original layout of the courtyard: "We would set up the tent in this corner." "What tent?" I asked. "The tent for *Sukkaus*. We ate our meals there." "And what did the neighbors say?" "Nothing. In those days, it was normal. Jews ate in tents during *Sukkaus*. Everyone understood and it was no problem. Of course, by 1944 we stopped. And after the war, it was somehow not important anymore. It would have been absurd in the spirit of the fifties." I was silent for a moment, then turned to him: "Whose idea was it to stop?" "It was not anybody's idea," my father responded. "It simply faded out of our lives. We were glad to be alive."

When I was a child, our street marked the edge of the district. Beyond it lay rows of one-story warehouses belonging to the parquet factory. If we continued in that direction for a long time, we reached my grandmother's house in the workers' district. From our apartment on the fourth floor, we could see the factory and a long stretch of the Danube with its islands. It was a spectacular view. A little industrial train pulled by a steam engine carried the wood from one end of the factory to the other; that is, to the corner of the street beyond our window. Sometimes I still wake up at night to the sound of a puffing steam engine. Every now and then, a horse-drawn carriage passed by our house and the clatter of hooves echoed off the walls. From spring to fall, the organ grinder made his rounds in the neighborhood. And at least once a week, the peddler appeared, shouting: "*Ószeres, ószeres, mindent veszek...* Peddler here, peddler here, I buy everything!" Strangely enough, she was a woman.

But in my daydreams, I imagined the peddler as a man. He was of medium height, dressed in brown pants and a jacket, and wore a hat. All in all he was rather elegant. He walked with his eyes fixed on the ground, as though he were looking for a hidden message in the cracks of the cobblestones. Although he looked serious, he was always humming a melody to himself.

In my dreams, we lived on the first floor of a house somewhat like my grandmother's in the workers' district. The windows were so low that you could easily step through them and out into the courtyard or, on the other side, into the street. One night, I saw my peddler sitting on the windowsill at the edge of my bed. With his back leaning against the frame of the window, his legs pulled up and resting on the sill, he seemed quite at ease. He was playing the violin, apparently for nobody in particular, since he did not notice me. The notes, a fine thread of silver, soft but firm, rolled out from under his bow. The thread flowed continuously, waving, curling and gradually filling the room. It reached the bed, curled around my body, my legs and hands, until I could no longer move. It wove itself around my ears and eyes, soft and suffocating. I screamed in horror. Nobody came. I was completely conscious and realized that my body still existed and that under the thread it was warm and that I was still breathing. I was overcome by a mixture of feelings of violence and gentleness, fear and submission—a confusion of emotions that made me cry. Tears streamed from my eyes, wetting the blanket around my face. Then, slowly, I fell asleep.

A few days later, I found him again sitting in the window. For a while, he came regularly. And something happened that almost never happens in my nightmares: I began to enjoy being frightened by his sad music. I knew that this was a dream and that I was not going to die. My heart began to beat faster whenever I noticed him, and I was certain that he was also aware of me. I imagined this was a dream that someone else was dreaming many years after I had died. Souls whom I knew nothing about and who were going to live in the future pleaded with me to weep for them. They squeezed my heart until I began to cry real tears, sobbing into my pillow. On empty nights when I could not sleep, I wanted him to come, perhaps even called him—so that I would be able to weep. When he appeared, I dared not move, fearing he would disappear. I waited in nearly unconscious excitement for the soft silk thread to wrap itself around me, all the while listening to his melody—the saddest, most beautiful melody on earth.

Then one day, he disappeared.

Secrets Padlocked Away

At the age of twenty-two, I began my ethno-musicological research among the Ortho-dox Jews of Budapest. It is difficult for me to grasp today the state of mind into which this work threw me. The feeling of awakening and excitement was mixed with bewilder-ment, shame and fear, as well as a sense of foreboding. My life's protecting walls began to erode, and the terrain that had been "home" was suddenly full of traps and barri-cades, creases and cracks that threatened with collapse.

It would have been easier to do fieldwork among a faraway tribe in Africa. For however hard I tried to convince myself of the contrary, the object of my research *was* my "tribe." It was easy to call them "religious" (while I am secular) and "uneducated people from some backward village" (while I am an intellectual from the capital); and I have no doubt that the capacity for clear-cut categorizations is one of the qualities required for survival when facing unanswerable questions. But for me, this did not work. I tried to focus on my task and make myself believe that it was a purely scholarly undertaking: the ethnographer collects strange melodies and customs. But wearing the costume of the ethnographer among men who could have been my grandfathers, I began to feel ridiculous.

It was not only the silent beauty of their religion—sounds of a life of withdrawal—that shook me, but the sudden intimacy with thoughts and attitudes so different from mine. Unknown objects and deep secrets, when I encountered them in my milieu, came from within my habitual setting; they were part of a world whose codes I knew and where I was comforted by proofs that my life was established. Amongst these people, I often felt as if in a hollow: everything seemed familiar, yet I recognized nothing. Sometimes my ignorance was funny, and we joked about it. But on the whole, it was like being in the wilderness: I was left to my instincts.

My research of Jewish music began because an American professor—unknown to me at the time—did not receive a travel grant. This professor, a German Jew by origin, lived in the Midwest. He had survived the Holocaust, escaped to the United States, and vowed never to return to Germany. But he could not do without his beloved Europe. He thought up an educational project for which his guidance was indispensable. He got the grant and spent the summer in Europe. The next year, he received it again, and from then on the money kept coming. Every summer, he raced through Europe, from England to Hungary (without setting foot in Germany), busying himself with his project. Then one day, the money stopped coming. He had to come up with a different plan.

Since his earlier project had involved Hungary, he knew important people there. As was well known, Hungary was the "happiest barrack behind the wall," and in the eyes of the American professor, he would be performing a valiant deed by testing the level of its liberalism.

He went to the main office of the Academy of Sciences to speak with an authority. Hungary lost six hundred thousand Jews in the Holocaust, he said. Hungary's great scholar, Bence Szabolcsi, the founder of Hungarian musicology, researched Hungarian Jewish music before the war. Even if there is much ethnological research going on in Hungary today, nobody studies the folk music of the Jews. The heritage of Szabolcsi has been forgotten. This is untenable. This is scandalous. If the Academy of Sciences agrees, he would be willing to initiate and oversee the research of Hungarian Jewish folk music. All he needs is a respectable local scholar to co-direct the project. Of course, they will also have to find a couple of students to do the actual job, but that should not be a problem. No need to pay them; it will be an honor for them to have been entrusted with such an important task. He will come every year to check their work. The whole thing would not cost the Hungarian Academy a penny. He will find a grant in America to pay his expenses. The authority liked the idea and suggested he turn to Professor Benjamin Rajeczky, who would surely be glad to co-direct the project.

The American professor talked to Professor Rajeczky, wrote the proposal and, in 1976, got his grant. Every summer, he returned to Europe, still avoiding Germany. Then, in 1980, disaster struck: the students who had been doing the job fled to the West. The professor was left without a workforce. The money stopped coming. I do not know what he thought up next.

His name was Alexander Ringer. If he were alive today, I would visit him with this book and thank him for his inspiring idea and intuition from the depth of my heart.

Professor Benjamin Rajeczky—or, as we called him, "Béni bácsi," uncle Béni—was a legendary teacher and scholar, a priest in a small town in Northeastern Hungary. I do not remember ever having another teacher like him. There was a wonderful atmosphere during his classes. Week after week, we conquered new territories, understood fundamental thoughts and attitudes of scholarship, music and life—all this happened without effort, as if *en passant*.

During the second year of my studies at the Academy of Music he called me into his office, along with Peter, a classmate of mine in the musicology department.

"My dear children, we have an important task for you," he began. "The late Bence Szabolcsi was not only the founder of Hungarian musicology. He also collected Jewish folk music and transcribed many folksongs. An American professor, who visits us every year, suggested that we, that is, the Academy of Sciences, continue his research. We have decided to ask you to take up this project."

It sounded like an offer from the mafia: a deal you cannot understand but must accept. *Who* exactly wanted us to do *what*?

"To tell the truth, I know very little about Jewish music," Professor Rajeczky continued. "It must be very ancient. It may even go back to antiquity, to the time when the ways of the Eastern and Western branch of Christian chant had not yet parted. It's related to this early Christian chant, and probably also to other oriental chants. The Hungarian version must be influenced by ancient Hungarian folk song. It's an interesting project. You will be able to prove these connections. This is very important for scholarship."

We were silent. We were both thinking the same thing: how did they find us? In the seventies in Communist Hungary, one did not pronounce the word "Jew," not even within the family, but certainly not in public, save for a few exceptional situations. To allude to the fact that someone was Jewish, God forbid, amounted to a crime against humanity. If anything, a person was "a Hungarian of Jewish origin," but calling attention to one's family roots was an insult. Our family did everything to raise us the right way. We were trained to speak and look like everyone else and avoid words like Auschwitz or Israel. We were not educated about Judaism. Hiding was in our genes. Yet, it was clear that our professors had picked us simply because we were Jewish. They must have gone down the list of musicology students until they found the first Jews. Of course, *we* had long since realized that we were the only Jewish students in the department. But how did *they* know?

"Yes," he went on, "I have to admit that I know very little about this topic. But I will help you in whatever way I can. I have already spoken to Professor Alexander Scheiber, the director of the Rabbinical Seminary. He said he would be happy to meet with you. Here is his phone number. As to the musical questions, the classification and typology of the melodies, you should work with the scholars Fazekas and Maros. And remember, you can always come to me. We will discuss the problems and try to solve them together. I will be happy to learn something new. Today I am alone in the office, but normally we won't be able to talk here, since I share this room with other scholars. But there are chairs and a coffee table in the corridor—nobody will bother us there."

(When, in 1989, after nine years in emigration, I came back from the United States to visit Hungary for the first time, I called Professor Rajeczky immediately upon my arrival. "Now we have a bigger office," he told me over the phone. "But they have taken away the table and chairs from the corridor. What wonderful hours we spent there! I hope you brought new pictures of your little son. The one you sent earlier is here on my desk. Is he still interested in percussion? Good, very good! You have to tell me about everything that has happened since you left. Come meet me in the Institute, I will take you out. I know a quiet place in the neighborhood where we can sit as long as we want."

That meeting turned out to be our last.)

After several months of waiting, the American professor appeared on a spectacular spring day budding with lofty promises. To his great regret, he had no time, he said; he had important people to meet. "But let's have coffee." We walked into a nearby restaurant that served international food. It took some time for the waitress to appear. "Sorry, sir," she said, "between noon and three in the afternoon, we serve drinks only with lunch." The American professor was outraged. "Ridiculous! Scandal! That's Communism for you! Everything regulated from above. In America, I can order whatever I want anywhere, anytime. What a shame we wasted our time on this stupid restaurant. Now I'll have to take a cab, otherwise I'll miss my appointment. I have an idea: come with me and we will discuss the project in the cab." In the cab, he mentioned a book on Jewish music written by a scholar named Idelsohn. "No, I can't send it. Besides, it's out of print. Ask a relative of yours in the West to find it for you."

While waiting for the miracle that would produce Idelsohn's book in Hungary, the musicology professors Fazekas and Maros advised us to read analytical studies on early Gregorian chant. "Perhaps your research will contribute to the understanding of the melodic modes of Christian liturgy," they told us. Professor Scheiber, on his part, suggested that we assemble a catalogue of articles on music published in the Hungarian Jewish periodicals during the early twentieth century, and intimated, by the way, that our presence was indispensable to his services and *Kiddush* meetings at the Rabbinical Seminary.

None of our mentors, not even Scheiber, suggested we listen to a service in one of the traditional Orthodox prayer houses. For Scheiber, scholarship meant evidence written down on paper—the older the paper, the better. But there could have been another reason: perhaps he wanted to protect us from conflicts with the police. After all, diligent work in the Széchényi National Library was less likely to attract the attention of the authorities than his students hanging out at suspect religious services. Or perhaps he did not know about the existence of those traditional *shuls* hidden inside apartment buildings all across Budapest. Or perhaps he knew about them, but did not think much of the crude and confused music practiced there. Whatever his reasons were—I will never know.

One could spend a lifetime reading about Gregorian chant. The number of Hungarian Jewish periodicals is not endless, but sufficient to keep one busy for long hours in the reading room of the Széchényi National Library. Thanks to my uncle in Israel, I finally held Idelsohn's book in my hands—a mildly worn secondhand copy. It contained a chapter about the music of the reform services, like those of the Rabbinical Seminary. But most of the book was devoted to an ancient and mysterious tradition. It spoke of music that sprung from the deep well of memory, nurtured by the breeze of desert dawn—music in which the heart's primeval ritual reverberated. I devoured these chapters. I looked up every unknown English word. I copied, hummed, memorized and classified the musical examples. I filled the margins with notes and analyses, then, at a second reading, erased everything and jammed new comments into every niche between and around the print.

I let myself be tossed from cliff to cliff over the abyss. Nobody talked about the abyss. Nobody looked me in the eye. The professorial glances were averted, fixed on the crystal clear peak of knowledge.

What is all this about? Where are these glowing and burning melodies on which such a horde of clever words is wasted? For what purpose is the wisdom of splendid libraries? Where are the dreams, the passions and the souls that had borne the music buried so elegantly in these chapters?

While ostensibly carrying out important research, I had an opaque feeling that something else was going on—that my entire being was at stake. My scholarly apparatus, cut off from my soul, went into action; it went to the National Library, studied Idelsohn's book, and made research plans with my friend Peter. It engaged in lengthy arguments about religious customs with Emmanuel, a student at the Rabbinical Seminary.

It discussed problems of melodic modes with professors Fazekas and Maros and had friendly chats with Rajeczky and Scheiber, who were always kind and ready to meet with us. Nobody knew how lonely I was behind the fences of scholarship.

One day, I gathered my courage and called the cantor of the Rabbinical Seminary. He was not particularly excited by the idea that I record him, but he agreed to meet me before the morning service on Shabes. I arrived an hour before the service started. I opened the large gate that led to the courtyard of an ordinary apartment building. I crossed the courtyard toward the part of the building that included the Seminary, and, on the second floor, the synagogue. The door was open. I entered and began to climb the stairs; my steps echoed in the empty corridors.

I knocked on the door of the cantor's private chamber and, after a moment, hesitantly turned the knob. He was sitting at the far end of a monumental carved wooden table. The walls of the room were covered with similar dark wooden carvings. His shining black robe and the somber atmosphere of the room weighed me down after the pure whiteness of the corridor. He was reading from a black, cloth-bound book and sipping steaming liquid from a purple thermos cup. He looked up and said, casually, "Oh, it's you. I can't talk to you right now, meet me after the service."

I returned to the corridor. I pressed my forehead against the window and looked out at the mist that veiled the scant patches of grass sprouting through the asphalt. A wall separated the seminary's narrow lot from the rest of the courtyard, and had it not been for the stubborn vegetation and the mysterious morning light, the view would have been distinctly oppressive. A thick layer of leaves streamed over and down the wall, thinning out gradually into a pattern of delicate vertical lines of leafless branches that reached to the ground. Above the wall, the view opened to a finely shaped, lonely tree that stood out among dark structures. The white mist of the morning light poured onto the landscape like brilliant dust from an extraterrestrial source, and the walls of the corridor inside the building echoed this morning radiance with their sleepy, greenish whiteness. I would not have traded this moment of resonating light for any music.

Suddenly, thunder broke forth from the cantor's room as he began his warm-up exercises: "Mimimimi, mamamama, mumumumu." I was suddenly overwhelmed by a tide of suspicion and embarrassment. I hurried out into the street, went home, and did not even call him to apologize.

Where did I get the idea that "this wasn't it"—that the music I imagined for the sound of Jewish prayer was not going to emerge from a resonant bass's *mimimimis*? I longed for a sonority that grew from the morning light on whitewashed walls, a vibration on the borderline of light and darkness, a whisper that stretched its wings above the yellow coziness of the gently lit halls. I had a feeling, dim and amorphous, yet clear as an axiom, that Jewish music should be the sound of its time and space.

I longed for this music I had never heard. I felt it whenever I looked at the photographs of my great-grandfathers, whose bearded faces were pasted onto the pages of our family albums. With bodies fixed in unreal, photographic poses, they focused on some enigma in the distance. Their faces made me uncomfortable at first, but the more I looked at them, the gentler they seemed, even assuming a touch of self-irony. For all their seriousness, they were immediate and somehow naïve. Although I knew that most

of them were learned men, rabbis or doctors, they reminded me of peasants. Their posture radiated closeness to the earth, evoking a reality of life in which the sole source of security is the ground beneath one's feet. The rest is told in sound.

∼ꝍ∽

Among the squiggly lines that the hand draws as the mind wanders between unformed thoughts, in the margin of one of my transcriptions, I found this sentence: "My first informant was an old man who refused to tell me his name."

"I asked Mr. Waldman to come over. He knows many old Jewish tunes," said Emmanuel. We brought chairs into a classroom in the seminary, placed the tape recorder on one of the chairs close to an outlet in the wall, and sat around the machine in a semicircle. Peter began the interview: "Please tell us your name and date of birth." "But you know my name already," Mr. Waldman answered. Peter pressed him for specifics: "Tell me also your first name. Where were you born? How old are you?" Mr. Waldman laughed: "How old?! Ha, ha! Well, I guess I'm over sixteen!"

He must have been in his seventies. I remember a small figure in shabby clothes, hesitant glances gone astray—a scruffy existence hidden behind the pretense of insignificance. Whenever I looked at him, images of Jewish peddlers came to mind. I remember his nonchalant evasiveness; with him, evasion was not an option, but an instinct. Whenever we asked something about his life, family, childhood or beliefs, he would shrug: "Oh, never mind! That's not important!" When, after the session, we offered to visit him in order to spare him the trip to the seminary, he replied: "Visit me? What an idea! There's no need."

(I would like to say the mourners' *Kaddish* for him, but I cannot be sure he is no longer alive. You never know with him; he was known to disappear and resurface unexpectedly in one *shul* or another. Is it proper to calculate the number of years? It sends shivers down my spine to think he *must* be dead by now.)

During the first meeting, Emmanuel did most of the talking.

"Please sing the *Borchu* for us," Emmanuel asked.

"Oh, that's impossible! 'Cause there are so many melodies, it depends on which day and which service and whether it's a Shabes or a holiday, and then there are different versions for *Raishashoni, Yomkiper,* and then *Peisach, Shvies...*" Mr. Waldman dodged.

"The one for Shabes..."

"But there's more than one for Shabes! It depends on whether it is morning or evening or..."

"Oh never mind, just do it, we will figure it out later."

"Now let me think, which would be the simplest."

"Not the simplest! We would like you to sing the original melody, the authentic melody, the one you normally sing."

"But when there are so many versions! *Are you aware* that it's different for holidays?"

"We would like Shabes, let's begin with Shabes! We're not interested in holidays; we have not taken out our *machzor* yet! Do you see a *machzor* here? So why holidays?"

"Ha, ha, that's good, if no *machzor*, then no holiday, that's really good! Reminds me of a joke, oh, it's a really good one, stop the tape, I have to tell it, ha, ha..."

Mr. Waldman, Peter and Emmanuel left together after the session, while I stayed behind to pack up and do a little work in the seminary's library. When the sound of their voices began to fade, I went to the window in the hope of catching a glimpse of them leaving the building. I waited for a while, but did not see a soul. The silence was complete; I heard only a gentle humming, as if the tape recorder's reels were still turning.

I rewound the tape: "Oh, that's impossible, there are so many melodies... Reminds me of a joke, oh, it's a really good one..." His teasing, joking words came back to me like some odd jabbering from a distant space.

I began listening to the melodies. Mr. Waldman's voice was ambiguous and whispery. It was ember and ash, the hollow sound of a chasm between infinite sadness and unrelenting embarrassment. It was a used, ragged, broken voice, a voice of exhaustion; torn shimmer behind dense smoke.

Instead of going to the library, I began wandering around the empty corridors, peaking into the classrooms, until I arrived at the assembly hall. I had been in this hall many times, since Professor Scheiber's weekly Friday *Kiddush* was held there—the only occasion when young Jews were able to meet. It was the single regular Jewish event authorized, or semi-authorized, by the police, for reasons that never became entirely clear to me, as Jewish public gatherings were otherwise outlawed during the Communist regime.

Such a crowd would gather here on Friday evenings that mostly only the elderly (among them also Mr. Waldman) were able to sit, while the rest stood jammed together in the narrow passages between the long tables. Each week, Professor Scheiber or an invited guest gave a brief lecture on a Jewish topic, after which the youth were allowed to do as they pleased, that is, within the limits appropriate for a gathering at a religious institution where, as was well known, there was no lack of undercover police. The religious aspect of the *Kiddush* was taken care of by Scheiber's quick blessing of the *chala* bread, after which—the room being so crowded that he could not move from his place at the front table—he performed his famous acrobatic exercise of tossing pieces of *chala* toward those whose athletic abilities he judged sufficient enough in order to catch them.

There was a wonderful atmosphere at these *Kiddush* gatherings, warm and welcoming—it felt like being part of a family. It often happened that, long after the *Kiddush* had ended, I would still be standing with a group of friends in front of the Seminary building, reluctant to conclude the discussion and part with the buoyant and optimistic spirit of the evening.

I entered the assembly hall, now empty and completely silent. The chairs were put up on the tables, and their legs, pointing upward, produced a sight of formidable orderliness. I was surprised to realize that this room was also a library, a fact I had not previously noticed amid the excitement of the Friday gatherings. Two walls were covered by book cabinets made of dark wood. The shelves reached to the ceiling and were filled with antique books in uniform, dark bindings, each marked by a number in white ink. The glass doors of the cabinets were padlocked. I walked around to check whether any

of them had been accidentally left open—in vain. I had never heard of this collection and had no idea where, if at all, it was listed in the catalogue of the Seminary's main library. The meticulous cleanness, the spotless, shining floor, and the neat order of this library of locked-away volumes made me feel uneasy.

As I was standing, perplexed, in a corner of the room, I dozed off and saw a bizarre apparition. It was Friday evening and people were crowded together under the soft yellow beams of electric light. The dream was voiceless like a silent film. Suddenly, Mr. Waldman appeared in the door. He stood there for a while, then made a hesitant step forward, and with a shake of the head walked steadily into the crowd of jolly youth. He carried a thick padding of white silence around him, and as he moved he cleared the room with his motion, bit by bit—the way a painter erases, with repeated brushstrokes, the deep, dark shapes of an oil painting, covering them with layers of uniform white and gray. I looked for the books on the whitewashed painting but could no longer see them; instead, there was a row of arched windows where formerly the cabinets had stood.

It took me some time to realize that I was staring at the reflection of the windows in the cabinets' glass panes. The mirage was so bright that one could hardly make out the books behind the glass, and I felt as if the library had suddenly opened up, allowing me to enter and fly through it toward other houses and windows, and finally, up to the clouds of the vast sky.

When later, at home, I listened again to the recording, Mr. Waldman's evasive laughter seemed even less real. His words resonated in my ears like an echo of nothingness. An empty and desolate courtyard. Lives and spaces that do not recognize one another. The feeling of having done something unforgivable has not left me ever since.

Rocks on the Landscape

I do not remember how I found Gärtner. He was the Torah reader in one of the larger synagogues in Pest. Every week, after the morning service, the *shachris,* he did the *leinen,* as it was called, the cantillation of the text of the Torah according to the precise rules for the melody for each word and accent. He lived in Miskolc, a large industrial town in Northeastern Hungary, and came to Budapest only for Shabes, taking the train on Friday afternoon and returning Saturday night. Since he was staying for Shabes in any case, he was entrusted also with the *mincha*, the afternoon service. The community paid for his travel, and naturally he was invited to all the communal meals and perhaps received some symbolic salary for his services.

"Shabes afternoon," he answered to my question as to when I could record him. "That's the best time; actually, that's the only time. After *misef* and *kidish*, I eat lunch. Then I have nothing to do until *shalashides*. I sit here alone the whole afternoon. You can come whenever you wish, nobody will notice."

"Oh, those tunes! I know so many of them, those wonderful, beautiful tunes from the old days. Like the *Ovini malkeini* from the *nile*. What a wonderful ... a splendid tune! The women were in tears when I sang it in my village. What, the women! Everyone wept, men and women and children—with real tears! Today? Where do you see such a thing in our days?"

I do not tell Emmanuel and Peter. I want to be alone with him. I come on Shabes around three in the afternoon. I stop for a moment in front of the door. Not a sigh can be heard from within. I turn the knob, he looks up, mumbles a greeting and sinks back to his solitude; his short, heavy figure towers over the open book like a heavy stone. This is how I would find him week after week—in a perpetual and immutable existence of withdrawal. I would never know anything about him, his memories, life and thoughts, save that on Shabes afternoons, in the loneliness of the study room, bending over books, he murmurs and whispers.

His singing is rough and jagged (a result of his heaviness, asthma and missing tooth), yet fired by enthusiasm. He begins by inhaling deeply. Then, accompanied by a whistling stream of sound as if being torn from an aching and throbbing substance, he propels heaps of melody-debris onto a vast imaginary expanse. He stops, suddenly. He glances at the text, vacuously silent, gazing far into himself, as if listening to the rustling from within, as if the new rocks in his throat were not ready and did not yet measure up to the mission of being flung out into the desert. But here he goes again: shooting his rocklings, as if he wanted to murder and crush, and yet at the same time, as if all this happened in parenthesis, along the way, as if it did not concern him at all. "Isn't it beautiful?" He does not wait for an answer. He liberates from his throat the next wave of sound-magma that, like those that came before, thickens in my mind into incomprehensible schemes, heaps with the odor of the earth in the depths of which roots and somber graves grow and catacombs blossom in indecipherable crossings.

"Nobody knows these melodies the way I sing them. None of this exists anymore. Either they make operatic flourishes, with ornaments everywhere, so you no longer hear the traditional melody, the *nisech*. Or they mumble, like those neo-Orthodox hippies.

No *nisech*, no music, just mumbling. It hurts; it is physical pain for me to hear how they trample on the *nisech*. In our time, where I come from... With me, it's different! One should *sing* the *words*, no messing around. Nothing matters, only the words, *each word with its melody*, and the *nisech* with its feeling—its atmosphere. The *nisech* brings its atmosphere. These are the basics, the essence."

"Here, is this prayer, for instance. Have we recorded it? What a wonderful, what a beautiful tune this is! The women wept when I sang it. And there was a cantor who came to our village sometimes especially for the *misef*, because, as you know, I'm not a cantor, just a simple *baltfile*. So he came sometimes, and he was a real cantor and could sing. Oh, how he sang! The women wept! What, the women! Everybody wept, men and women and children!"

I have no idea what I am recording. I can barely decipher the Hebrew letters and know nothing about the prayer. His explanations resonate in my ears alternately as gibberish and shamanistic charms: *misef-nisech-baltfile, ovi-nimal-keyni, tara-rara-rara-ra, tara-tara-raa-ra.*

He keeps on with his scheme relentlessly: "Oh, this! I must sing this for you. This is a wonderful, a splendid melody! The women…" "Excuse me, uncle Gärtner, could you tell me please on which page of the prayer book this text is?" "This? This is the main prayer on *Yomkiper*! Of course, you don't go for *shachris*, that's too early for you, isn't it? Most women show up only for *misef*, they honor us with their presence around ten or eleven. But, I beg your pardon, this is in the *misef*, this, pardon me, is the most wondrous and splendid text and it is heartbreaking. Remember how many times you have shed tears on these words! Just think a bit, you know this, of course, you know, because you go to the *misef*, although not to the *shachris*, because the women…"

He persists. He takes no notice of my imploring looks and questions. He does not give in to the fact that I know nothing and have never been to a Yom Kippur service or to any other holiday for that matter. When I ask a question, he raises his head and looks at me with bewilderment—it seems rather as though he were looking through me. He waits for a while, then lowers his glance and goes on mercilessly with his prayers.

My Gärtner epoch was a journey full of ambushes. The realization of an unknown existence began to dawn—not exactly on or even inside me, but rather in front, behind, below, beyond and above—an existence at once near and unattainably far. It filled my heart with terror, and yet exerted such a powerful attraction on me that I feared I might lose myself in it. I was standing at the edge of a crater and had to hold on with all my might so as not to be swallowed by the swirling heat, while at the same time, secretly, not admitting it even to myself, I would have been ready to descend and disappear in the depths.

I had never asked myself what religion was. In those days, for us, in our twenties, religion was finished business, a useless past that belonged to old people. But dietary rules, the observance of the rituals, and the commands and restrictions of the holidays are not a matter of belief or ideology. They are more like the air and the sun, an atmosphere that grows into one's life—it becomes one's skin, hair, bones and eyes, smiles and sorrows. I have no recollection of ever having decided that I remain an atheist, or the opposite, that I become religious. I do not remember having said to myself: "From this day on, I will not travel on Shabes because, according to the rules of the Jewish religion, traveling on Shabes is forbidden." I rambled across the boundless terrain of a life-perhaps-to-be-lived; a secret existence burst into view like a mirage between the sky and the earth, I walked in and out of it effortlessly, as in a dream, and the mirage remained, limpid and pure, solid and stable, and time went its way calmly and without demands.

I do not know how it happened, but from a certain moment onward I found myself in the prayer house every Shabes morning. Of course, I walked there; I could not have imagined taking the tram or the bus. In order to gain a broader view of the Jewish customs, I decided to visit all the still functioning prayer houses in Budapest—according to my plan, a new *shul* each Shabes morning—but this, as I soon realized, was impossible. Even though I made every effort to ease the congregation's discomfort, by announcing my visit beforehand and dressing in the most conservative manner possible, my appearance at a *shul* where I was not customarily seen always created an atmosphere of apprehension. They were at a loss as to how to speak with me and how much of their intimate ways to let me notice. The service became unnaturally subdued and at the same time, somehow theatrical. "We have never seen you here, who are you and what do you want from us?" they would have liked to ask, but they preferred to remain silent. It is best to ignore the intruder and, in any case, one should not talk too much. Since I was already there, I went through with it, but in the end I fled the scene with a bitter taste in my mouth. I had destroyed the serenity of their prayer.

For me, too, such visits harmed the idea of Shabes, turning the day of rest into a draining and hazardous expedition. After a period of wandering, in the course of which I did in fact visit several of the functioning prayer houses, I settled for a pattern of alternating among the few where I felt I was tolerated and sometimes even welcomed.

But my wanderings continued even after I had settled for my prayer houses and become familiar with the route that led me there. I drew labyrinthine paths and tangled detours, intricate and confusing zigzags on the map of my mornings, spending hours on the cold and dark streets, in dazed and aimless vertigo, as if not being entirely certain that I was destined to arrive at that place, or anywhere else.

I cannot say what I expected from these Shabes walks. Whatever my notions may have been, they opened up a capacity in me to see and understand things in a completely unexpected way. I was on the streets at dawn, when, in winter, the streetlamps were still lit. The houses seemed abandoned and enigmatic, and in the mysterious fluidity of dusk, even if I walked on familiar territory, it seemed I was wandering in a foreign land. These early morning walks became a wordless ritual whose meaning needed no explanation.

On these wanderings, when winter light flooded the deserted streets, I would never cease to be amazed by the perfection with which formerly bourgeois Budapest, whose buildings were adorned by myriads of magnificent and fantastic decorations, had been turned into a landscape of impoverishment and decay. A thick layer of dust obscured any trace of the original colors, and at any moment plaster ornaments would break off from the wall, hitting the asphalt with a thump that sent a chilling echo through the deserted streets. Hastily put up signs, often on both sides of the street, advised those who cared for their lives to walk on the opposite side.

Well, that's how we are. I was talking to myself. These buildings from the late nineteenth century, these poor things have gone through a lot indeed! How *should* they look after what they had to put up with? These walls had endured the destructive impulses of several generations; they survived sieges, airstrikes, battles, dictatorships and liberations, demagogies, manipulations, famines and poverty. They were witnesses of the apocalypse. These dumb windows with their dodging silence had seen it all, swal-

lowed everything and kept silent. They are fatigued and worn out and no longer believe in anything.

In the nineties, a new fashion swept across Europe, and since then, no town with any sense of pride can do without a facelift. Historic city centers have been mercilessly invaded by boutiques and jewelry shops and by an insatiable urge to enhance the effect of the makeup with vivid colors. In the seventies, this was not so, not even in Western Europe and certainly not in the East. The murderous signs of the war and the following decades were everywhere, and in the cracks of the asphalt of deserted lots roses of misery blossomed.

For those of us who were brought up in this era, this network of signs meant home. Those who had not lived in such an environment did not know how talkative and even humorous the signals of decay were. I did not know whether to laugh or cry at the sight of a façade from which every bit of original decoration had disappeared, revealing a set of rusted metal rods that looked like pegs for hanging coats in some school gym for giants.

But for the most part, the decorations were sufficiently intact to allow one to reconstruct the original pattern, and the curious blend of beauty and decay provoked the imagination. The dwindling buildings struck me as sincere—the way people, music and stories are sincere when they are not immediately comprehensible. They were like reflections on water, yellowed paper surfacing from a cellar's musty boxes, diaries whose pages shelter the secret of your life—if only you could read the chirping of the birds whose flights are hidden between the rows of letters. The streets were like books waiting to be deciphered, their stories restored. That is: they were real books—books whose meaning you penetrate only on a second reading, when reading them for the second time is really like reading them for the first time.

These houses taught me more about research methods than any university course. The exercise in reconstruction and imagination prepared me for my descent into the secrets of long lost worlds: I realized that the essence of things becomes transparent precisely when they are on the verge of disappearing. I understood that the discovery of the unknown is an imaginary dialogue with the unknown—a conversation whose basis is empathy and fantasy.

The landscape was not dead. On the contrary, it gave the impression of a burgeoning empire that had recently been conquered by knavery and deceit, machinations and bold tricks. The new inhabitants, many of whom ascended to these apartments from poverty-stricken villages, slums, lagers and other habitats of misery and despair, accepted the majestic overflow of decorative plaster ornaments with unperturbed indifference. They were unmoved by the beauty of the buildings, which they felt, probably with reason, was not meant for them. Haunted and martyred, and with a chilling determination to defend it, they clung to the minuscule hole that was, so to speak, theirs, and for which they would have let themselves be torn to pieces, and which they themselves tore and scratched and butchered and mangled, breaking walls and building new ones, fencing off corners and alcoves. The ruins of these evidently endless projects lay around like pieces of a grand puzzle in pavements and courtyards, in the landings of stairwells and at the entrances of basements and attics. I could never understand why a nicely proportioned window frame was fitted into a decaying wall, which, in turn, was adjacent to another decaying wall; what a sofa was doing at the entrance of a building next to the neglected, though otherwise beautiful stairwell, and why dozens of tin buckets were left out in an empty lot until they froze in the icy snow.

As there were very few cars and the streets were silent, the passerby was let in on the lives of the inhabitants. Sounds coming from behind the walls became companions in my wanderings. I took note of the development of the children practicing their pillow fights; I knew where the quarrelling couple lived and who turned up the volume of the radio punctually at seven for the morning news.

Walking on one sleepy street, whenever my journey took me there, at seven in the morning, I could perceive a peculiar sonority coming from one of the ground-floor apartments. It was the sound of a typewriter, that unmistakable *pirit-pirit-put-put-pirit* of reverie and amazement, which I often heard at night from the direction of the elevator shaft. I had never found out who sent those Morse codes from behind the wall of my bedroom. When I myself was laboring on seminar papers sometimes as late as two in the morning, we went on exchanging our thoughts in quest for the meaning of life, a riddle that we forever solved through the alternation of our rhythmic polyphonies and anxious silences—the most complex philosophical arguments.

That year of early morning wanderings produced my most elusive thoughts and memories, and whatever I wrote about them, whether then or years later, fails to convey even the remotest impression of my curious, mystical apparitions. I can recall one image with some clarity, perhaps because it occurred on the route I traversed countless times in order to visit a secluded prayer house.

On my way, there was one street with a huge antique gate of heart-rending stillness. I was drawn to that gate, as if by a spell, pushed it open and entered. On the right side stood a two-story building with a row of narrow windows and entrances, whose humane proportions struck me as a memento from a long lost era—as in fact it probably was, the building having been modeled on a country house, its porch substituted by the central courtyard. In the back and the front, lonely wooden constructs, which had served for the dusting of carpets before the era of vacuum cleaners, stood like skeletons offering their bones to the birds to sit on. The small house, with its grayish white wall, seemed utterly displaced among the jumble of windowless brick walls.

For reasons I cannot explain, this desolate courtyard provoked in me a sense of protection and serenity. One radiant morning I spent almost half an hour standing there. The patches of gleaming grey-white snow reciprocated the whiteness of the sky, and

it was so strangely silent that I could hear the sighs behind the walls. I was frightened when, in the back of the yard, a group of pigeons suddenly took off. I involuntarily overheard a fragment of a conversation, which I remember to this day: "She asked her mother to lend her a hundred forints so she could buy food for the children. Mancika said she would be glad to, but does not have that much herself."

By the time I arrived at the prayer house on the second floor of a decaying structure of a similar courtyard, the service had already begun. I crossed the courtyard, climbed the stairs, and entered the apartment. I was about to turn the doorknob of the prayer room, but I changed my mind. I remained in the antechamber, motionless and silent, listening to the murmur of the prayer filtering through the wall. It seemed I had finally arrived at *my place*: the threshold between inside and outside—a space undefined and yet entirely safe.

The sound of prayer flutters, soars and slithers, enters and hovers, looks around and nods, then purring and whirring, splashes its way in and out of me. In its waves trembles the mirage of a barbed wire fence, coral forests of burned lives emerge and the canvas of deepening visions wells up in disembodied dimensions. Now suddenly (who knows how and why) the sorrow dissolves; the prayer's sonorous river smiles away the tears and the arms of its waves begin to rock those long dead minutes and lives. Because those minutes and lives had not died. Listen: they are here, suspended in time, vibrating and beaming, weaving their perpetually crossing fibers of wondrous dreams, reverberating in eternally inchoate memories; it is they who hold my pen and carve these lines into the air in a forever withdrawing mysterious *now*.

After these emotionally draining morning walks, which were sometimes followed by a service in an unfamiliar prayer house, it was a relief to spend Shabes afternoon with Gärtner. But the evening once again brought hours of anxiety, as I struggled to describe the contents of the session. I put the tape recorder, prayer book, paper and pencil on the table and listened to the first item I recorded that afternoon. I memorized the beginning, trying to make sense of the words, then searched for it in my prayer book, the *siddur*. When it seemed I had found the text, I listened to the recording in an attempt to match it with the words in my *siddur*. It often happened that the first few words of an item corresponded to the words I found in the book, but the continuation was different. I went on searching.

One day, I spent the entire evening looking for the text of a prayer, combing through thousands of Hebrew letters. It was after midnight—I kept only the small desk lamp lit so as not to disturb my parents sleeping in the adjacent room—when it finally showed up, on page five hundred thirty-two. I was in tears. They were tears of fatigue and desperation—but also of shame.

There were not many options for Judaic studies in Hungary in those days, but if one looked hard, one could find guidance. I could have turned to my father. He had attended the Jewish Gymnasium before the war; he must have learnt the prayers there. I could have spoken with some of the seminary's students; I knew them from the Friday *Kiddush* gatherings. I could have asked Bence, the most trusted of my friends from these circles. He was an intellectual *enfant terrible*, devouring languages, living and dead alike.

A few years older, he already had a doctorate in Romance languages and spoke six of them fluently. One day he submerged into the inner group of the Kazinczy Street synagogue. He absorbed religion with the same speed and sharpness of mind that had characterized his linguistic undertakings. Then he disappeared. I would not see him again until a chance encounter many years later, in Budapest, where he had returned after long years with the community of the Satmar Hasidim in Antwerp.

I could not bring myself to turn to him or to anybody else. I did not want to learn to pray as if it were a subject at school. I wanted to learn it as *they* did, by doing it, hearing it, being lost in it, being carried away—praying, getting lost, stumbling, praying, getting lost, stumbling—the same circles over and over. I did not want to "take it in"

as material assigned for an exam. You should not do that with prayer. You have to let it live, settle, take root, breathe and grow. Without arguments and explanations. Today, I know that it was madness. Whenever someone tried to help me—when Emmanuel, for instance, offered to identify the pieces on my tapes—his words tore my skin. One cannot be taught *one's essence*.

After all, it's not so difficult—even a child can understand. The basis of the Jewish ritual is the text. Every service has its set of texts: one for weekdays, another for Shabes, and again different ones for the many holidays—a tremendous mass of text, but, fortunately, with overlaps. During the service, your task is to open the prayer book at the beginning of the text assigned for the given occasion and read it to the end—all the lines and words, one after the other, as they are printed in the prayer book—whether it is a psalm, a blessing, a medieval poem or fragments from the Torah or the Talmud. Whatever the text, you go on reading and reading and don't skip anything. That's all. You have to be able to read Hebrew, of course, and fast, extremely fast, since the prayers are long and if you stumble or daydream, you will not reach the end.

Throughout the service, you read for yourself in a low, melodic voice, but if you are not there yet or the melody does not come to you on that particular day, simple recitation suffices. The others in the prayer room do the same; they all murmur the prayers to themselves. From the moment you enter the prayer house until the end of the service, you hear the gentle murmur of prayer all around you, all the time.

The *baltfile*—that is, the man who leads the prayer—reads the same texts as the rest of the community, murmuring his melodies like anyone else. But here and there, he steps out into the light, so to speak: he raises his voice and gives it color, making the recitation more musical and melodious. Until now his voice was inaudible—but suddenly he sings and proclaims and leads. This change from murmur to melody signals that we have reached a particular point in the prayer—usually the end of a section. The people understand: those who were behind with their reading now speed up and those who ran ahead stop and wait. The *baltfile* knows his community; he knows what tempo is good for most of them.

Depending on the prayer and its liturgical function, the rules might be different. For instance, the *Shemone esre* demands that everybody says the full text in a silent voice— so silent that only the person praying hears his or her own voice. The *baltfile* does the same: he completes the prayer without raising his voice. After everyone has finished the silent recitation, he repeats the text with melody. During this sung repetition, people do not murmur; it is not necessary, since they have already said the prayer. They are free to listen to the *baltfile*, or, as some seem to believe, to chat with their neighbors. Another prayer with a particular rule is the *Ovinu malkenu*. Here, the *baltfile* sings and the congregation repeats the text and melody line by line. And there is a unique prayer, the *Hineni heoni* of the High Holidays. It is the personal prayer of the *baltfile*; he alone sings the prayer, while the congregation listens.

I am learning rule after rule as they come up in the sessions with Gärtner. He does not care much for the murmuring parts; instead, he sings sections where the *baltfile* is prominent. In the actual service, the *baltfile* usually sings the first words of the prayer, announcing its beginning like a fanfare. Then he lowers his voice and murmurs together with the congregation. Close to the end of a section, he raises his voice and sings the last few phrases with a melody. This ending sounds like a self-contained unit, a minuscule song, a pearl in the sea of murmuring. An accomplished *baltfile* does not stop at the end of the section or even pause to take a breath, but continues straight into the proclamation of the beginning of the next section. And again: after the first few words, he abruptly stops singing and submerges into the murmur. The result is that the melody for a word toward the end of a text (the first word sung with voice) strikes one as a beginning, and the melody for the beginning of the next text sounds like an ending. Those who do not know this do not realize that these melodies, which strike one as perfectly shaped and full-fledged tiny songs, begin with the end of a text and end with the beginning of another.

Evening after evening, I sit at my desk with the tape recorder and prayer book in front of me. In my book, it is not always clear where a section ends and a new one begins. Even when it is clear, I cannot be sure whether Gärtner is not skipping a section and picking up at a completely different place in the service. Even if this is clear, I cannot know where he begins within the prayer—how many lines before its end—and whether it is the beginning or the middle of a sentence. When the prayer is among the "famous numbers" of the High Holidays, I can find my way relatively fast, having referenced and cross-referenced the recordings of these pieces. But Gärtner will often jump to any prayer at any time regardless of the order of the service.

I listen to the tape and identify the word *shpliroi*—or is it *shpiliroi*? By method of elimination and other additional tricks—I have developed a sense of ease in navigating several hundreds of pages of text—I arrive at the *Hallel* prayer, which is composed of a series of psalms. Had he sung the opening blessing, I could have found the text relatively quickly. Instead, he skipped it and began with the first psalm—that is, with a word in the middle of a sentence near the end of the first psalm. The text reads *hamashpili lirois*. The tape preserved only a passionate *shpliroi*—a heavy sigh.

After a few months, it often happens that when Gärtner begins a prayer, I faintly remember having heard the text before. I begin to look for it, frantically leafing through the prayer book. He stops, waits, loses patience and, with a deep sigh, launches into another one of his *shplirois*.

One afternoon, after we have finished recording, Gärtner turns to me: "Why don't you stay for *shalashides*?" *Shalashides* is the communal afternoon meal—the last ritual meal on the Shabes. I excuse myself and explain that I am expected at another *shul*. "But you go there every week, why can't you stay with us once?" he begs. I am hesitant. "What are we going to do with the tape recorder?" It is forbidden to record on Shabes; we have been carrying on with our sessions in secret. He suggests we hide it in the closet. I give in and stay.

I am here only for Gärtner and do not know this community. There are quite a few young people. I glance at their faces, trying to decide whom to talk to, but I have no strength to start a conversation. I badly miss my usual hour of rest between the recording session and the *shalashides*, the walk home and the walk to another community. Having no better idea, I go to the corridor to look for the toilet. As I am about to return, a slim man in his thirties blocks my way. I try to go around him, but he grabs my arm and whispers in my ear: "Get out of here! We know you, you work for the police, you filthy spy!" I am speechless. I free myself and go back to the room, my heart pounding. I feel the blood rushing in my ears, pulsing on my lips. I sit down on a bench in the corner, too scared to move.

One of them sits down next to me: "Are you all right?" I do not know what to say. It feels as if this were a film. He does not wait for an answer. "Don't worry, he's nuts. I know what he said to you. He told me before he went after you that he thought you were a spy and that he was going to throw you out. The truth is, we have never seen you here and you don't look Jewish." I feel faint. Is it really that simple—if you don't look Jewish, you're a spy? And how can this guy be sure that I am *not* a spy?

"Oh, it's no big deal!" he continues. "We're all spies. Look around: who's not a spy in this room? Do you think there is anyone here who has not been to the police station at least once? When you are there, you cannot fool around, you do what they want, you have no choice."

I recover my voice: "What do they want?"

"Well, as a matter of fact, not much. They want to know all kinds of things about people you know from *shul*. For instance, they put a photo album in front of you with pictures of the people from *shul* and ask what you know about them—that kind of thing. Of course, you do not dare deny ever having seen a person you sit next to every week. Because *he* might be a spy," he says, his voice entirely calm.

"And then?" I ask.

"Then you have to listen to some trash about how we Jews always stick together and how that's no good. Usually that's all. Sometimes they take your passport."

"What?"

"They take your passport and you cannot travel anymore. Just dare try getting it back! You will get no answer, nothing. Sometimes they create a bit of a mess for you at your workplace. That's about it. They don't beat you or the likes, at least not that I've heard. But they can do nasty things, like what they did to the guy who wanted to throw you out. That was not nice, to put it mildly. This is why he is always so nervous. To tell you the truth, he was not completely normal before. I have known him for a long time. By the way, I am Robi."

I am exhausted, but Robi seems to be enjoying the topic. "They weren't exactly polite with me either. Want to know what they did to me?"

"No," I answer.

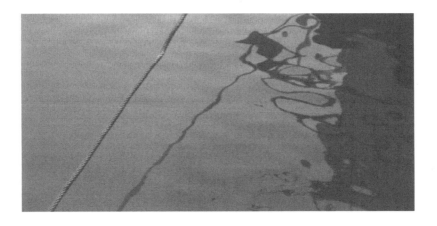

"I won't insist, but in my view it's good to share information so that you know what to expect. *Because, sooner or later, you'll end up there, too.* That's how things are."

I wish I could go, but I need my tape recorder. I look at my watch—*mincha* should begin any moment. Finally, everyone except Gärtner leaves the room. We take the tape recorder from the closet. I am free to go at last.

At home, I tell my parents I have an errand and don't know when I will be back. I go down to the Danube. It is a beautiful summer evening. I find my place on the stairs. I could sit here and look at the waves forever. This river and this city are my home. I watch the reflection of the ropes—lines curling, bending and weaving themselves into glinting patches of light that reflect off the waves. The thought that I will leave the country is like a steel pin in my heart. My heart is cold; it will never get warm again. My brain is paralyzed—I do not need it any more. My whole life condenses into a small, bright point on my retina. For the first time, I feel I have lived and have a past. No, I cannot leave. It is impossible. My nerves are woven into this soil; they are nourished by these houses, these people, this language and its poems, these concert halls and theaters, and everything else, good and bad. My parents. My grandmother. Life makes no sense elsewhere. I make no sense elsewhere. I wish I were as strong as Gärtner. I wish I could tear my heart out and spill my fears, heaps of molten lava-sound, onto the grey desert of my future.

I stay at the Danube until I begin to doze. I cannot bear the thought of going home and facing my parents with the seed of betrayal in my heart. No, I won't do it—I have neither the strength, nor the heart.

I wish somebody would come, take me into his arms and carry me away. Away from everything—to begin anew, like in a fairytale.

Gärtner was my mentor and professor. He ignored my ignorance and gave me no guidance. He did not point at the text in my prayer book. He assumed my book was open on the right page and that my constant looking down was a sign that I was following the text. He explained nothing and pretended not to hear my questions. His patience was inexhaustible, his endurance made of stone. He protected me, and my many masks, but made it clear that he expected me to be there every Shabes. Between three and five, he mercilessly flooded me with his prayers.

After some time, it began to dawn on me that, from the hundreds of pages of prayer texts, he chose a few dozen that he sang over and over again. His favorites were from the *sliches* and the other services of the High Holidays. I recorded *Adoinoy, adoinoy* and *Ovini malkeini* at least five times. As the weeks passed, I devoted countless nights, hundreds of hours, to disentangling the words. I still knew little, but I was no longer nervous on my way to *shul*, and felt at home in the study room. I was able to perceive the change of light brought on by the approaching autumn and smell the High Holidays in the air, although I had not yet been to any. He was patient and I was patient. I asked nothing. Quietly, diligently and conscientiously, I recorded whatever he sang. Then, one day, I could not take it anymore.

"Now, since the holidays are approaching, I want to sing something special for you, the *Ovini malkeini* from the *nile*."

"We have recorded that already," I say, annoyed.

"Oh, really?" he puts down the *machzor* and looks at me with wide eyes.

"We have recorded *Ovinu malkenu* several times," I insist.

"But not the one for the *nile*. What a wonderful—a splendid melody! The women wept…"

I interrupt: "We have recorded it several times. It's the same melody for *shachris* and *musaf* and *nile*, the same for *Roish Hashono* and Yom Kippur."

"Really?" he asks, taking off his glasses. "Well then, let me think of something else. Perhaps it is time I translate a text for you." He lets out a gigantic sigh, straightens his back, goes to the shelf and comes back with a holiday prayer book, a *machzor*. He flips through the pages, stops and puts the open book in front of me: "Look at this text. It's the *Akdomus*. Have you heard of it?"

"It's for … I think, for *Shavuas* … I mean, for *Shvies*," I say hesitantly.

"Indeed. The first day of *Shvies*. Or *Shavuas*, as you wish, it's the same thing. Hmm… So you have heard of this. Well, it's a very difficult text and I am going to translate it for you. Or at least I'll try. Now turn off the tape recorder, would you…"

Our few remaining sessions were different. There were still no questions and no answers, but, at my request, he would now sing complete services from the first prayer to the last, without skipping anything—just as he would in the prayer house. We finished recording Shabes and moved on to the holidays.

Then, one day, I found the study room locked. I inquired after Gärtner and was told that he had been hospitalized and that it would be a few weeks before he came back. None of the people in the synagogue knew his address, and they suggested that I contact the Jewish community in his hometown. I sent a letter, but got no answer. I wrote again, and made another round in the community. People shook their heads. They did not know his address or the hospital where he had been taken, but assured me that there was no need to worry, because he had just called the day before. He was all right and would be back within a few weeks. I can wait a few weeks, I thought. I never saw him again.

Silver Thread

In memoriam Jenő Roth
Chayim Binyomin Ben Ha-Rav Shmuel Rotha

I start the tape recorder.
"Shall I begin?" he asks.
"Yes," I say.

"Shall I begin with *Ashrey*?" He is hesitant.

"Yes," I reply.

He prays. He finishes his prayer. He raises his head from the prayer book and looks at me.

What am I doing here? What am I doing here—an ethnographer spy sneaking into another person's clandestine existence? Who am I to be manufacturing scholarly arguments from shattered memories? What business do I have, sneaking around in a life I should be living? And if this is not the life I should be living—then what, indeed, am I doing here?

My notes from the course "Methodology of Ethno-musicological Research" read as follows: "Before interviewing the informant, the ethnomusicologist should prepare a questionnaire designed to obtain the data necessary to establish the origin of the melodies, their function, and the influences and interchanges among melodic genres and types. Where did you learn this melody? Whom did you first hear it from, and when? Did your father and mother sing it? Did you hear it from others? Did they sing it the same way? Do you know another text for this melody? Do you know another melody for this text?"

I discuss the results of my research with my professors. I follow their advice and continue my study of Gregorian chant and Hungarian peasant music. I join a choir that performs Christian chant. I memorize Hungarian folk songs. They are beautiful. The folk ballad that begins with the words "Mother, dear mother"—which I have transcribed in great detail, down to the smallest fluctuations of rhythm—is engraved in my mind and moves me to tears even today. I come across a recording of oriental chanting. Countless plays have nearly erased the hills and valleys on the surface of the Supraphon record, which bears the title *Oriental Origins of Christian Songs—an Anthology of Documentary Recordings by Dr. Leo Levi.*

The issue of influence is the cardinal point of our thesis, my professors say. The primary task is to demonstrate the interchange between Jewish melodies on the one hand, and Gregorian chant, oriental singing, Hungarian folk music and the music of the surrounding ethnic groups on the other. My research should prove, my professors say, that Jewish music, as a separate culture, does not exist. Every music culture is but an expression of the eternal and universal laws of music; in the same way that "Jews" themselves do not exist: they are merely part of mankind. Furthermore, Judaism and Christianity have common roots. The music of both religions originates in Oriental chant. This is what needs to be proven: the oriental origin and the influences, particularly the influence of Hungarian peasant music on Hungarian Jewish chant. And the influence of Christian chant on Jewish music. It is common knowledge that Jewish culture is not "pure"; it is a mishmash of whatever Jews found among surrounding peoples.

Darkness descends upon my mind. The professorial arguments are my food, but it is indigestible. The loops of twisted logic close around my brain and I shudder to think that behind the scholarly arguments, in the dark alleys of the subconscious, suppressed aversion lurks like the green light of witches' curses.

Chayim Binyomin Ben Ha-rav Shmuel prays. I make an effort to listen analytically, recalling what I have learned in class, in the choir and from records. My thoughts frantically search for the model of his melody—it must be hiding somewhere in the boisterous swarm of melodic fragments in my head. I jump from the Ethiopian recitation (collected by Leo Levi—who is this Leo Levi? I wonder simultaneously) to a Gregorian antiphon to "Mother, dear mother" and to more distant melodies and fragments whose sources I no longer know. I force myself to recognize all or any of them in Chayim Ben Shmuel's prayer. I must be able to establish the origin of this melody in another culture. Remember, the cardinal point of the research is influence. Argue. Demonstrate. Here and there, I snatch a sliver of melody from the air. I fold it, squeeze it, until it becomes similar to another melodic scrap in the jumble inside my head. I am not convinced. I need to listen more systematically. My nerves hurt from concentration, but the more I concentrate, the more the spider's web of melodies closes in on my mind. Sometimes, it seems as if all the melodies are the same—born from a single primeval mother melody. At other moments, nothing reminds me of anything.

Chayim Ben Shmuel prays as if I were not there. Bent over the prayer book, his eyes on the words, he chants his prayers with an eternal, lulling melody. He finishes a text and begins the next one without stopping, without even looking at me.

It feels as if he weren't singing at all. An alien voice blows through his body, it sings and drinks him, inhales and exhales, and an airy and immaterial, silent and serene, timid and delicate silver thread seeps through the rocks—and tranquility enfolds us.

But in the depths of tranquility, within the apparent plainness of the notes, a wilderness of suppressed passion stirs. It expands into amorphous universes, splashes through obscure mazes of underground veins, flows toward distant horizons on which serpentine watermarks wither away and are reborn. It descends in somber downpours and expands into gigantic waves that swell, bubble, multiply, until finally, in the cascade of notes, the forgotten language awakens—the *sound-for-the-no-one-and-nothing*. The stream rushes over me, and my mind is engulfed in flames. I sink. Deep in the serenity of the sea of prayer, empty and voiceless, at last my burning mind cools.

Chayim Ben Shmuel looks up from the prayer book. I cannot speak, I feel as if I am under water. My mouth asks the questions. He hears them, attempts an answer, stutters and stumbles, then loses the thread and falls silent. He waits for me to say something. I am speechless and he is puzzled. His eyes search for something to look at. He looks down, then out the window; he leafs through the prayer book, closes it and turns it over, then kisses it and puts it back on the table.

The apartment consists of two spaces: a kitchen that is the antechamber and also contains a makeshift shower, and a room that serves as the couple's salon and bedroom. The toilet at the end of the open corridor is shared with the neighbors. We occupy the salon during the recording session, while Chayim Ben Shmuel's wife waits in the kitchen. The room is crowded with old-fashioned furniture, dark surfaces strewn with a collage of diverse objects: porcelain figurines, piles of paper, a comb, brushes, a medicine holder, vases, a doll, an ashtray… The wall is painted with a dense, fading pattern of wavy flowers. A crystal vase with red and yellow tulips, which Chayim Ben Shmuel bought for the occasion of our first session, has been pushed to the edge of the table in order to make space for the tape recorder. In the windows, a grayish-white curtain of knitted arabesques provides shelter from the sun. The curves and curls multiplied in the knitted lace spread over the headrest of the armchairs. My tears flow back into my eyes as I take in this exuberance of undulating sorrow.

Chayim Ben Shmuel looks at me. His face shines with kindness and resignation. His hesitant smile asks forgiveness—only he knows what for.

"Where did I learn this? Well, first of all... I don't know because ... because I did not learn this. I've been praying since I was a small child, since the time... I don't remember a time in my life when I wasn't saying the prayers. In the yeshiva we didn't deal with such things ... with the prayers, because we knew them already. It would have been quite bad otherwise, really bad—not to know them, I mean—because they are the prayers. I'm from Hajdúnánás, but when I was still a young boy I was sent to Bodrogkeresztúr—that's where I had my *barmitsve*. Then there was the *lager* ... the *lager* ... yes ... and then forced labor ... and all the rest..."

"First came Miskolc. I learnt a lot in Miskolc, Talmud and *nisech* and *chazunes* and other things ... but not prayer. There was no need, because we already knew, like everybody else from Hajdúnánás, of course... My mother, how could she not know! She sang the prayers with melody, how else? The moment children began to speak, they were saying the prayers. Perhaps even before. With their melody, of course..."

"But not everyone brings out the melody as clearly as I do. Because the way I do it … that is my personal melody, the original and authentic melody. It's the same all over the world, at least in the Jewish world. This is how people in my village prayed, because we had a traditional and deeply religious community. People prayed with devotion. No, not devotion, that's the wrong word, it's not devotion like in church. With us, there is no such thing where you just stand and stand and say nothing, just meditate in silence. With us, there is always *davenen*… the whole time and it never stops … this *davenen* … do you know what it means to *daven*?"

"So when did I hear this melody? I don't know, I really don't know. Because it's not like you hear a prayer from a certain person at a certain year and then start singing it. Everybody had been singing it before. It had been there since… I don't know exactly, but for a very long time. And everyone sings the prayers for those same melodies in the same way. No, actually, not the same way, because everybody sings differently, according to his ideas, the way he feels, the way he is able to live through the text … live through it. I mean those who pray with feeling—which means concentration. We say *kavunes*, but here in the city, the moderns say *kavvanah*. This is the most important thing, to pray with *kavunes*… Do you know what that means, *kavunes*?"

He falls silent.

"I don't know these things. I am not educated. As a child, I was already a *chazzn*. In those days, people thought I was talented, that I had a special talent for Talmud and a nice voice, which means a talent for *chazunes*. I was taken in by the *tsaddik* in Bodrogkeresztúr and Miskolc, and also by the *chazzn*. They taught me for free, which was almost unheard in those days. Today I don't speak about this. It interests nobody. When I was nine years old, I was already teaching the older boys."

"But the questions you are asking, Juditka… Such questions never … how shall I say … never arose. We never spoke about dates and melody and origin. Only one thing mattered: devotion, *kavvanah*, *kavunes*. The *kavunes* brought out the melody."

He stares at the ground and his hands play idly with the prayer book. He speaks of devotion and concentration—of *kavvanah*, *kavunes*. I have come to establish melodic types and devise scholarly arguments.

I wish he would go on talking. I cannot explain why the inconsistency of his explanation does not bother me. Not understanding its precise meaning, I am listening to the melody of his narration, and it is enough. His Yiddish accent, the many unknown words and the gentle hesitancy of his speech evoke an atmosphere of serenity and warmth; the sound of his voice unfolds in my mind like flower meadows with the fragrance of grass and air.

He waits for me to say something. I cannot speak. The lucidity and precision of my phrases would be unbearable. He stopped singing only a few minutes ago, and already I feel empty. I want to travel on the river of his prayer, be carried away by the waves. I want to be wrapped in the cotton soft silver thread of his voice.

My clever questions, what do they know?

With a voice that is not mine, I thank him for the session and begin to pack my things. He smiles. "It's a great thing you're doing, Juditka. It's a *mitsve* to record these old melodies. Come again next week … any time."

I returned. With time, I learned to ask less. One day, Jenő Roth, whose Hebrew name is Chayim Ben Shmuel, began to teach me.

"I want to explain three things. If you don't know them, you won't be able to fulfill your responsibility in prayer. So I will explain them to you now. These three things are *davenen*, *nisech*, and *kavunes*."

"*Davenen* is prayer. It's the simple prayer you say every day, three times a day: morning, afternoon, and evening. When you *daven*, you say the words, I mean, read them as they are in the prayer book. That's all you do, nothing else. You say them to a tune, of course—it would never occur to anyone to say the words without notes. You could do it without melody, I suppose—the way they read at the university—but this was not the custom where I come from. In my time, in the villages, and not only in the villages but everywhere in the Jewish world, prayer, learning and reading … all these things happened with melody. Still, it's not a song. You don't *sing* the prayer. *Davenen* follows the text as you feel it, according to your rhythm and your voice. In some circles they call this what you call it, Juditka, *recitation*. I heard this word here in Pest for the first time."

"The most important thing is not to add anything or stop or make unnecessary flourishes and ornaments. You have to read fast, very fast. No, actually, that's not what matters, it's not the speed, but that you should not stop, not even for a moment, just go, simply, without breaking it, you go with the words. What you feel is your business—it's a personal thing. And even if you don't feel anything, when you have a day or a situation when you are unable to give yourself to the text, even then, you have to say it. You have to say the prayers for their sound … for the sound of the words. *The words should sound for you every day of your life*. Nothing but the words and their sound. In *davenen,* you do only what's essential."

"This is how it was in my village: we, the children, got up at four in the morning and went to the *cheider* to *daven*. It lasted until six. Then we ran home and had a quick breakfast, because we had to be at the public school by eight. We studied until about noon. By one o'clock, we were back in the *cheider*. There, we studied mostly the *Taire* … the Torah. Not prayers, because we knew those already. We had been saying them ever since we started speaking, even though we did not understand the words—for as you know, the prayers are in Hebrew and we spoke Yiddish. Nobody translated the prayers and nobody explained the meaning, so for us, in the beginning the prayer was just the sound of the words. But slowly we figured out their meaning, and when we began to study the Torah in the *cheider*, we came to understand them more precisely, because words from the Torah and the psalms surface all the time. The *cheider* lasted until seven in the evening, but if the material was difficult, which happened often, it did not end until nine. Then we prayed and went home."

"Where was I? Yes, the second important thing is the *nisech*, or as they say it here in Budapest, *nusach*. When you pray for yourself, you may *daven* to whatever tune you wish, whatever melody comes to mind. But when you pray for the community, when you lead the prayer, when you are a *baltfile*—or, as we used to say in my village, a *shliach tsibbur*—you have to follow the *nisech*. Each prayer has its own way, its own *nisech*, which means that it should be sung with a special melody and style. But every *baltfile* has his … how shall I say … manners … or versions … because you are free to do it your own way, as long as you keep to the basic rules. If you manage to stick to the rules and still do it your way, with your personal ideas and feelings, then people will say you have a beautiful *nisech*. But this is not easy. You have to know exactly what you are allowed to do and when—and not every *baltfile* can do it."

"But when you are a *chazzn*, or as they call it here, a cantor—when you improvise— you don't need to stick to the *nisech*. You have to know it, but you don't have to sing it; it's enough if you think it and be ready to return to it at any moment. Because … now, let's open the prayer book … take this prayer, for instance. I begin this prayer with the simple *nisech* melody, because I want to let people understand what is happening. In the second line, I begin my improvisation and it's no longer the *nisech*. But I have the *nisech* in my head, even though I don't sing the notes. Then, in this line, I come back to it, and then, in the next line, I improvise again."

"The essence is that even when I do not sing the *nisech*, I hear it in my head; the basic melody is there all the time, in the background. And if the *hazzn* does not return to the basic *nisech* melody even once in the whole prayer—that's good, too. Actually, I don't have to come back to the *nisech*; I do it only for this community, so that people will see that they have a *hazzn* who knows—a *hazzn* who, whatever he might do, will always be able to return to the simple Shabes or holiday melody. But if I pray in a community that is religious, the way we were in the old days, a community that really knows the melodies and the rules, I don't have to give this kind of … how should I say … reminder. In such a community, the *hazzn* is free to go wherever his ideas take him. Now, if someone who knows nothing whatsoever about these things enters the synagogue and hears what's going on, that person would say, 'This cantor doesn't have the faintest idea of what he is doing and what the *nisech* should be.' But those who understand and have the melodies in their ear would know that even though not one note of the *nisech* is heard, the cantor knows it all, it is in the back of his mind, and his melody has the soul of the *nisech*."

"And they will also hear that this man davens every day. Three times a day, as it is written. *Nisech* and *davenen*—that's the essence. If you know the *nisech* and you *daven* every day with *kavunes*, people will hear it in the way you sing. But it's not simple."

"A good *hazzn*, and even a simple *baltfile* should be able to do everything, every *nisech* with its melody and style, and the variations. *Davenen*, *nisech*, improvisation— but that's not all. He has to know songs, and be able to compose new ones, because there are certain texts that do not follow the *nisech*, but a song. And it's the tradition to introduce songs at such texts, interesting and expressive songs, both old ones and new."

"A *hazzn* has to have a repertoire. He has to learn the compositions of the great masters. We called him *hazzn*, but here in Budapest they say cantor. A young cantor should memorize these compositions exactly the way they were handed down to us, because these pieces have been tried in practice and become tradition. Then, when he is ready to stand in front of his community, he may add his own ideas and improvisations. Or he may leave the piece as he received it—that's his choice. I was lucky because I had great masters, first in Bodrogkeresztúr and then in Miskolc, where I went to yeshiva. I learnt a lot in Miskolc. You cannot do these things without a teacher, a master."

"A good cantor should even be able to sing like they do in the opera—with a big voice, and expression, I mean … *their* kind of expression, because it can happen that he functions in a community where that is what is needed. When I was young … have I ever told you this … I was invited to perform at the opera. Perhaps I should have accepted."

"A real cantor has to know all these things. He has to know the styles, and be able to move between them very fast. That is the custom. Each part of the service has its own style. A good cantor *composes* his service; he shapes it according to the custom, with taste, and with his own ideas and feeling."

"What else did I want to say? Ah yes, *kavunes*, *kavvanah*. This is the most important. *Kavunes* is devotion. It's … compassion. No, no … not exactly… It's more like will … no, not will either … rather … concentration. I don't know how to explain it."

"It means that when you pray, you focus on the meaning of each word. With all your might, with all your mind and heart, you concentrate on the meaning, only the meaning. Take, for instance, the word *mimkoimcho* in the *Kedishe*. It means, 'from your place.' This is the first word of a sentence in which we ask *Hashem* to come to us from His place—the place into which He withdrew from this world. This world that is around us these days… When you sing this text, when you read it, you have to imagine this secret thing … the place where He hides His face from us."

"No, that's wrong, the way I'm saying it. Because you don't imagine it, you shouldn't imagine these things. It's rather that you concentrate on that place He will appear from—from far away, below or above. No, no, this is wrong, too, you don't do this with the text, you don't … how should I put it … define it in your mind, explain it in colorful ways and put all kinds of everyday images onto it. When you sing the prayer, you have to hold on to the idea—not the word itself, but the essence of the idea behind it. You have to concentrate on this essence and feel it, only it, without fantasies and explanations. That is *kavunes*."

"Let me tell you a story that will help you understand. I was the youngest child in our family, a late child. Then another boy was born, my little brother. I was very happy, because until then I had been the youngest and everybody took care of me but nobody took me seriously. Now I also had somebody to take care of, and I could say, 'What a sweet little baby,' just like the grown-ups. I adored him. He died soon after he was born; he probably wasn't even a year old. I don't remember exactly, because I was still very small myself."

"I could not accept the fact that I had lost him. I went to the cemetery to look for him, even though it was forbidden; my parents forbade me to go there alone. As I was walking among the graves, I heard a voice. It was the voice of an angel. It hovered in the air, somewhere high up, on a few notes, very clear and fine, high-pitched notes, like the sound of a flute. It was like a flute but even more ... I don't know how to say it ... tender. It went on and on and did not seem to want to end."

"It was so beautiful that I had to stop and listen. This has to be the voice of my little brother, I thought. It did not make sense, because he was too small to sing; all he could do was cry. But his soul must be able to sing, I thought. I was such a naïve little boy—I thought what I was hearing must be coming from the soul of my brother. I have to find that voice, I said to myself. I was afraid, a child alone in the cemetery, no small thing. But began to search anyway. The voice pulled me forward like a magnet; it called on me to follow. It was not easy to find, because the sound was coming from all directions as it echoed off the gravestones."

"Finally, I found it. An old man, with a long white beard, was praying next to one of the graves. When he noticed me, he turned towards me and I saw that the skin on his face was smooth, without wrinkles. His face shone—it was the face of a child. At the same moment, he stopped singing. It was terrible, that silence, as if the voice had been cut off with an axe. It was then that I understood that my little brother had died. I was terrified and ran home. It wasn't the sight of the old man that had scared me, but the silence when he had stopped singing. That silence terrified me ... that thing ... that sudden nothing."

"A few days later, when I had calmed down, I tried to remember the melody. I couldn't. This was strange, because it was a simple tune, just a few notes. I was certain that I would remember it. I had a good musical memory, and had already memorized some difficult prayers. But this tune ... I lost it. I lost it forever. It was the most beautiful melody I ever heard."

"Wanderer, stop for a moment …

… and accept that the terrain of your existence is nothing more than an intuition which never unfolds, and find comfort in the thought … that all we hold to be true … is unrecognizable in its labyrinth of hollow beams…"

(Zsuzsa Beney, *The Möbius Band*, translated by Ben Niran)

Once again, I am at the entrance to his apartment building. I enter the bolted gateway and begin to climb the stairs. I think of my mother climbing these same stairs and multiple other similarly filthy stairways on her daily rounds in the district. She is the family doctor of this poor and largely Jewish neighborhood. She knows everyone who lives in these apartments without toilets, buildings without elevators. She comes weekly to distribute prescriptions and to do the few things she is able to for the elderly tenants who,

at the first sound of steps on the enormous open corridor, with a concerned look peek out through the window of their cramped kitchen.

I hear the sound of plaster beneath my feet. I reach the top floor. I stand in front of the door. Will it be the same today, me asking my stupid questions? Sitting in the armchair exasperated and dumb? I feel I have nothing to offer.

"Juditka, it's good you're here… That tune, the one I talked about last time, it came back to me, I remember it now. You know, it's easier for me to remember these things when you're here, when we speak, because it's been a long time since I heard them. But I have it now, the one I learnt from my master in Miskolc. It's a special tune. My master … when he sang it, he was *there* … at the other place, that place beyond. Now, come in quickly, my wife baked some pastries for us, it's kosher, that's how we are, we eat kosher, it's really good you came…"

I wake up at five in the morning. The moon is whistling in the courtyard. The windows are asleep; I am the only one awake. I listen to the scratching sound of my pen as it scrawls silence upon silence. The white shame of my questions and hesitations piles up in my windowsill. What was I doing there, pretending my heart was not melting? From the black hole that swallowed them up, melodies flow back into my ears, my mouth, my veins.

… The ecstasy of his *Borich habo* in the *Haggadah* …
… The sorrow of *Tsur Yisroel* in his *nusach* for *Roish hashono* …
… The silver thread of his *mincha*: *Ashrey* …

I am cold in the silence of a night without miracles. Let my freezing fingers, holding the pen, murmur their soundless prayers.

"It is possible to pray in such a way that no other person can know of your devotion. Though you make no movement of your body, your soul is all aflame within you, and when you cry out in the ecstasy of that moment—your cry will be a whisper."

(Hasidic saying)

"Mendel Singer prayed. He knew his prayers by heart; he prayed mechanically. He did not think of the meaning of the words; their sound alone was sufficient. God understood what they meant."

[…]

"Mendel Singer […] lighted a candle and began to sing one Psalm after the other. He sang on good days and on bad ones. He sang when he had thanks to offer to Heaven, and when he feared it. Mendel's swaying movements were always the same. And only from his voice an observant listener might perhaps have recognized whether Mendel, the righteous, was thankful or burdened with anxiety. In these nights fear shook him as the wind shakes a tender tree. And care lent him her own voice; in a stranger's voice, he sang the Psalms."

(Joseph Roth, Job: The Story of a Simple Man)

For countless nights during those years, I stayed up late, leafing through books that would disclose the secret of *davenen*—offer an explanation as to why these sounds, so hollow, lacking any musical sophistication, reach terrains deep below what we believe we possess inside ourselves. Whenever I read poems, novels and essays about Jewish life imbued with *davenen*—Hassidic tales, Joseph Roth, Isaac Bashevis Singer, Aharon Appelfeld—the words breath an air of silent bewilderment. We all have our unique paths to the realization that we cannot make sense of the things of the world. My path was this research—what Chayim Ben Shmuel's was, I know only vaguely.

After I emigrated, we lost contact. I left Hungary illegally and was a refugee in the United States—to receive a phone call from an illegal expatriate might have been dangerous. An ambiguous feeling of having missed something, of not having lived up to a task—an urge to correct a past mistake—never left me. Wherever I went, the magic of his voice remained with me. The knowledge I had accumulated, the vast surfaces I covered across the continents—nothing mattered; I was forever searching for its secret.

I remember a hot summer afternoon in our Upper West Side apartment many years after my emigration. I am standing by the window and roll up the glass pane, and think of the hours I spent with him. The heat is unbearable. The broiling air seeps into my pores. The rumble of the air conditioner is like the vertiginous flight of a nightmare escape. A truck howls in a delirium over the scream of an ambulance and a madman is writhing on the pavement. In the stream of running bodies, nobody seems to care that the ground is trembling.

I move away from the window and sit down on the soft carpet. My transcriptions are laid out before me like enormous maps. I start the tape recorder. My head throbs and I am weighed down by the darkness of the approaching evening. I listen to his *Kedusha* for Shabes *shachris*. I recorded it after he was released from the hospital. His voice was gone. In some parts, he could not even hold the pitch. His singing was frail and uncontrolled, but emotionally, he could still do everything.

He begins with a grandiose display of scales and figurations—the operatic voice proclaims a heroic sounding melody in major. In the next section, he moves on to a florid fantasy in minor, using the flexible voice and style typical of the Eastern European *hazzn*. I sit on the carpet, bewildered, sweat pouring from my body. I do not understand. I do not understand how he can move so effortlessly between styles that are so different emotionally and musically. Half of what he does is tasteless kitsch—these cantorial exuberances, for instance—and the other half, depth and mystery—*davenen* and *nusach*.

For me, that is. For him, these assemblages from different styles are simply life. "A good *hazzn*, and even a simple *baltfile* should be able to do everything. *Davenen, nisech*, improvisation—but that's not all. He has to know songs … and have a repertoire of pieces… He has to know all kind of styles, and be able to move between them very fast."

I listen to the recording. I come to the central part of the *Kedusha*—or, as he used to say, *Kedishe*—which begins with the text *"Mimkoimcho malkeini sofiya"*—"From your place, our king, appear." I listen to it for the hundredth time. I pore over the transcription. I pace across the room with the music in my head. What is this? The melody is simple, the combination of a minor third and a major second. In a slow, gentle and lulling rhythm, delicate circles are drawn with the permutation of merely four notes: a leap up to the third, then to the fourth, then a descent to the tonic, then up again—the miniature melody is bending and curving, pulsating and swaying without ever stepping over the limits of that tiny space it carved out for itself. So different from the cantorial flourishes that came before. Why the sudden change? This is not song. But it is not *davenen* either, nor is it *nusach*. What is it then?

I need a break. I press my forehead against the window and try to take in the infernal theater parading on the street below. In New York, I am never homesick—there is no need. Manhattan streets have the capacity to expand to immense proportions, gobbling up everybody and everything. A vast supermarket prairie, populated by all imaginable forms of madness, is there for you to pick and choose from. I draw my fingers along the cool windowpane. I feel the dampness in the air. The colliding noises cancel each other out and there is silence in my ears.

Suddenly, I am overcome by a terrible, desperate yearning. As if I were standing on the edge of a crater, the earth slips away under my feet and I sink and sink, spinning myself out of existence. The feeling is so strong it hurts. Then, a melody emerges in my ear—his melody. My heart melts with longing, and after years of self-imposed decorum, for the first time, without self-pity and shame, my tears begin to flow for the never-was-never-will-be home.

I come to my senses. I go to the bookshelf and take out the *Sefer ha-niggunim*, a collection of Chabad Hassidic songs, and open it onto the chapter *Niguney ga'aguim*—songs of longing. "In Miskolc, at the Hassidic yeshiva, we sang melodies that long for … I don't know how to say it … for that … for that place. *For Him.*"

I read the music and hum the melodies. Now I know. Roth's melody for the text *Mimkoimcho* is a *nigun ga'aguim*. He had to burden the first part of the *Kedusha* with a display of vocal garlands and shallow emotions, place all that is superficial in front of you, only to annul it with one gesture and draw you towards the only thing that matters.

No, that's not it. I have to accept the beauty of the cantorial style. You have to take in everything, the heterogeneous objects, emotions, melodies and existences that come your way, so that you will be able… Let's try again. In the first two sections of the *Kedusha*, he placed all that is exuberant and beautiful in front of you, only to annul it with one gesture and draw you towards the only thing that matters: *longing*.

The longing of a man for his faith—the years of his youth spent in spirituality. Longing for a life swallowed by the flames. Longing for the master. Longing for the Place. For Him.

I search among the songs in the collection. They are similar, but none of them is as moving as Roth's melody. They are real songs with a beginning and an end—with a self-contained structure. Roth's melody is an "almost-song"; the beat is approximate, the phrases are haphazard, and the melody is minimal, like a paradigm. "From your place, appear"—a melody of dim light, a mere sign, a sigh, a gesture of yearning. An embryo dreaming that it will come to this world in the form of a song.

I go back to the window and look outside. I gaze at the windows of the building on the other side of the street as they light up one by one. I enjoy watching the street, this puppet show, this grand macabre spectacle of an eternal fair, this vibrating and glittering kaleidoscope of shattered lives.

He died a few years after my arrival in the United States. My mother is on the phone. "I just wanted to say," she begins, but I hear only noise at the other end of the line. "What?" I shout into the receiver. "Well, just that Roth died. Jenő Roth, do you remember?"

I hang up. I am numb with the realization that in the midst of the struggle for career and survival, I had forgotten what was most important. A question mark fades into the distance. A thread without end, an unfinished sentence, a cloud in my brain that never cleared up. I took a photo of him once, when he was already very sick. He is sitting on the bed with the prayer book in his hands, and stares into the camera with an embarrassed look. "Juditka, why should we record this? What's the point?"

In my dream, I visit him. As always, he greets me with hurried gestures, as if he has something to hide. He mumbles a rushed greeting with a smile, and quickly closes the door behind us. "I'm so glad you came." He tells a joke and then launches into complaints about the Jewish intelligentsia, while making space for the tape recorder on the only table in the only room in the apartment. I connect the wires, check the equipment and look up at him. Opposite the microphone, sunk deep in the armchair, he sits with his back bent, his eyes fixed on something in the distance, with an expression that frightens me. I am shocked by the change from the man who told me a joke a minute ago, to the one who is now sitting at the table—a stranger. Our channels no longer connect. I know that if I were to ask something now, about melodies, musical rules and customs, he would stumble on incomprehensible half-sentences, tongue-tied and hesitant.

He opens the prayer book. Chayim Ben Shmuel prays as if I weren't there. He never looks at me. The prayer book in his hands, his eyes on the letters, he recites text after text. Without beginning or end—the sounds pour from above, around and beyond, rain and snow and river. With an alien voice, the text sings itself. Withdrawn into the unknown, unconscious and unaware, he allows the words to *sound*. I no longer seek understanding. I only want to be… I want to be nothing. The gates of heaven open and I am lost in the brilliance of fleeting resonances.

Music?

My grandmother seemed to know that when I grew up, I would do something with music. The thought did not leave me. I was still at elementary school when I ventured, secretly and on my own, to a distant part of the city to see the Academy of Music— an expedition that seemed to me as dangerous as the discovery of the North Pole. I walked back and forth in front of the building, almost worshipping it—even though the grandiose façade and the empty windows impressed me as something forbidding, hollow and monstrous.

I came to know music through routine: the endlessness of the minutes as they cohered into hours, days, months and years in the thoughtless sloping of fingers on the keyboard. Precious times from my childhood; hours of boredom, self-torture, irritation and anger on the alabaster keys of my piano. Conscientious and disciplined, I did as I was told—practice, practice, practice. With the pieces I had been practicing for months I no longer needed to concentrate on what keys I touched; my fingers kept moving, my mind was numb.

One day, as I was playing a piece for the hundredth time, I was overcome by a sense of ease and transparency. A chill ran down my spine. For the first time, I *heard* what I was playing. As if a door had been flung open and I could step inside a previously unknown and mysterious, yet light and playful dimension. My eyes stared at my fingers touching the keys of the piano as if on their own, while I heard a story that came from another planet—from deep within.

Was it the same for the Jewish children in Eastern Europe? Like mine, their road led through repetition and practice—the long hours of mechanical *davenen*. It is said that the journey toward the moment of transcendence is like a flight on an unending spiral—whirling, vertigo, forgetfulness—and at the same time a surrender to the tyranny of perfection.

I do not know, nor do I understand, but something inside me does not let go of the feeling that we walk the same path in myriad incarnations. The long hours of practicing and, later, researching, transcribing and analyzing all served the single purpose of recapturing the feeling I lived through as a child—the moment when things become real. A realization that flares up like a sparkle and vanishes in a twinkle—that second is worth everything. For a moment, life becomes transparent in the sounds—I *am* the sounds.

When, in the prayer houses, people told me not to record someone because, "It's true, he has nice melodies, but he is not *in the prayer*," I knew exactly what they meant. "Being in the notes" is something else than understanding. What could a twenty-year-old music student, which I was at the time of my first recording sessions, have understood about Beethoven's tormented life, Mendelssohn's search for a place where his strangeness could be set free, or the mystery of Jewish prayer in which belief in life coexisted with the realization of its loss? Sounds work their magic in a muddled way. The mystery lies in accepting the invitation to descend into the soul's underworld, the catacombs of unnamed pasts and alien existences: to search, in the dark, for the other, and through it, for the self.

I first became conscious of this *essence* in music during the summer I spent playing and conducting in the school orchestra of Maestro Charles Bruck. He was my uncle twice removed and the only musician in the family. I was sixteen when I first met him during one of our trips to Paris, where he lived, years before I had started my work on the Jewish prayers. Charles—or "Karcsi," as we called him in the family—asked me to play a piece on the piano. I was even more nervous than usual—it was no small thing to play for one of Europe's greatest conductors—and naturally, I played badly. He said nothing; he just nodded and invited me to study at his school in Maine, in the United States, the following summer.

Charles had an enormous repertoire and his quest for perfection was legendary. He conducted the premiere of more than six hundred modern works in France and could hear every voice and notice the smallest mistake in an orchestra of sixty musicians. He had the technique to conduct anything and the heart to unearth the hidden layers of emotions. He remained himself and he remained inside the music, candidly and uncompromisingly, until the end of his life. When people, especially famous people, grow older, they tend to put on a mask: they begin to "play" their now petrified character. Charles was incapable of doing this. He was always himself and lived fully in the moment.

Talking about emotions was not part of the curriculum at his school. The rehearsals were tense, like some sacred rite whose practitioners know that the neglect of a single detail would cause the stars to halt in their spheres. Charles demanded that we pay attention and live through the meaning of each detail with utmost concentration and all our might. Only the notes and the instructions of the score—the essence. I remember a rehearsal with Michael, one of the best students, conducting Debussy's "Nuages" from the *Nocturnes*. I can still see the baton trembling in his hand. I am afraid he will drop it. We come to the seventh measure. Suddenly, Charles rises in his chair and bursts out: "*Pianissimo!*" His face turns red and his body shakes as he screams. Michael tries again, but when we reach the same measure, the little man in the back jumps up again: "*Pi-*

anissimo! Piaanississimooooo!!!' The students glance at him worriedly. We were seriously concerned that one day he would get a heart attack during a rehearsal.

A few hours later, I am sitting with him on the porch of his house. I watch him doze off, his fingers resting on a cup of afternoon coffee, a drop of dew sliding down from the brim. I dare not move. It is heartbreaking—the tenderness of the moment when an old man falls asleep.

He suddenly opens his eyes and smiles at me.

"Why do you shout?" I ask him gently.

"Me? I don't shout." He is surprised.

"How can you say that? You always shout. And that's not good. The students are afraid of you." I try to make him understand.

"When did I shout?"

"This morning, for instance, you shouted '*pianissimo*' during the Debussy rehearsal. It should be *pianissimo* all right, but why can you not say it kindly? Michael was almost in tears from fear."

He looks down and says nothing. I cannot believe that this is the first time someone brought up his shouting. "I don't want to frighten anybody, and certainly not Michael. I really don't," he says, breaking the silence. "But I can't bear it. It hurts. There is no melody in that measure... More precisely, the English horn ends its melody when it appears... Some color, something barely perceptible, an atmosphere... brilliance. One does not *play* this chord; it's simply *there*. The people in the hall should feel a chill running down their spines; they don't know where this is coming from … this apparition. When we approach this measure, I can already hear the sonority of the chord in my head, the airy sound of the flute, the horn in *sordino*, then, the timpani tremolo and the violins, *divisi*, in the high register. I feel the sound in my bones. I feel so close to him… I know what it meant for Debussy to compose this magic. And then this young lad, whom by the way I like very much, comes and tramples on it with his idiotic, lazy *mezzo forte*. It hurts; it is physical pain for me. I scream because it hurts."

In the evening, as I pass his room, I notice that the light is still on. I knock and enter. He is sitting at his desk, cutting his fingernails, a score lying open in front of him. I know this is how he works: he does something unimportant and mechanical while the thoughts take shape in his mind. I come closer and notice that it is Brahms' First Symphony. He has conducted it countless times, and at rehearsals he does not even open the score.

"What are you doing?" I ask. "Do you need to study this?"

"Don't be so loud. Look, here is that little insertion, four measures altogether, but I never understood what it meant. I have conducted the piece many times and we got through it somehow, but in reality, I never knew what was going on, what these measures were supposed to be. This is no theme. But it's not a transition either, nor is it an interlude. What is it, then? I think I finally get it. Leave me, I need some time alone."

Another evening, I find the score of Mendelssohn's *Die Schöne Melusine* on his desk. I look at him with an expression of surprise. "No," he smiles, "*this* I really don't need to study anymore. But it feels good to leaf through it. What do you think of this melody? It's the theme from *Rheingold*, of course. But when you check the dates, you realize who stole from whom. Wagner stole this melody. He put it into his generator and whipped it up, and now people faint in delirium. But it's not so simple. This piece by Mendelssohn… Yes, indeed, it's a bit timid and apprehensive. He does not quite know what to do with his big emotions, or perhaps whether he is allowed … whether one should … whether one ever … ever will be allowed to speak of those things. Like wind touching the river, causing it to tremble."

"It's a matter of taste," he continued. "To tell you the truth, I prefer music that has a bit of humility. Music that is not entirely sure that it is at the right place at the right time. Music that stumbles…"

"People have no fantasy," he said to me another time. "You go to a concert and it's so predictable: a symphony with four movements, then the next symphony with four movements, and so on, with applause in between. Berlioz once wrote in a letter that he thought of performing Beethoven's *Third Leonora Overture*, the 'Scène aux Champs' from the *Fantastic Symphony* and the 'Scène d'amour' from *Romeo et Juliette* in one concert. This would mean a concert with the *Leonora*, which is a love story, followed by two love scenes—nothing else, just these movements, one after the other. I thought of conducting this program for the second part of our final concert."

"When these three movements are played together, you have an entirely new piece, the movements of which do not proceed towards a solution, according to a dramatic plan. The movements stay in one place—and that place is … love. There is no finale. It would be impossible. No conclusion resolves longing."

"There is nothing in life apart from love. We go about our important tasks with serious faces. But it's all just child's play. In the end, nothing matters. Nothing matters but love."

"The students have asked me to let them record the concert. Out of the question… You cannot record a concert. A concert is like a love letter. Love exists in the moment. When you read a love letter addressed to you, your tears flow and your heart breaks. But when you read your great-grandfather's love letter to your great-grandmother, it might perhaps be interesting, but it sounds alien and even a bit embarrassing. Those outmoded figures and flourishes! And your grandchildren will feel the same way when they read your love letters. In devotion and feeling, which are the only important things in life, there is only present tense."

"In order to be in the music, first you have to…"—but he did not finish the sentence.

"Besides, I don't like recordings. They don't interest me. People are so involved with the dead that they don't have time for the living. They forget to look each other in the eye. I don't care if I am forgotten after I die; I don't even mind if my best concert is forgotten. In fact, this is how it should be."

The profoundness of that last concert effaced the residues of all the frustrations and failures, the heaviness and sorrow that had amassed in our hearts during the summer. Everything was in place: the energy of the orchestra, the baton, the atmospheric pressure, the concentration of the audience, and the constellation of the stars. At that moment in the "Scène d'amour" when the theme returns *forte*, Charles turned to the cellos and sang the melody together with them in a full voice. Then I saw him do something he had never done before: he gestured as if he were tearing his heart from his chest. Nobody noticed. The peculiar thing was that after the concert, each of us remembered it differently. We all swore to having seen or heard something that nobody else remembered seeing or hearing. Our eyes and ears of that evening, together with the notes and passions, flew into the outer spheres, to be swallowed by the dark, eternal cosmos.

I came back from Charles's school filled with an enormous enthusiasm for music. I realized that I was not going to be a pianist, and most likely not a conductor, either, and I was not sure what I wanted from music. But first and foremost I had to study and listen, study and listen. Already during my first year at high school, apart from the playing I did at home, concerts were the most important thing in my life. Now I felt it was my task—almost a moral duty—to be in the concert hall every night. Even though concerts were cheap in those days, I could not buy many tickets. Fortunately, a classmate explained that it was not necessary to have tickets at all, because the third floor gallery was reserved for students of the Academy of Music, who got free tickets for the seats there. It was not difficult to sneak in, he explained, and this was preferable not only because you did not have to pay, but also because there, nobody dressed up.

At the third floor balcony, a woman called Irma was the usher, and her task was to check the tickets. "I am a student, but I forgot my ticket," I told her. She examined my face and my tidy, long braids: "You?" "Yes," I said, "I am in the musicology department." "You?" she snapped. "Enough of this nonsense, can't you see how many people are waiting—get inside, will you?" I did not understand what she wanted me to do, but I entered the hall anyway.

Even if you were alone, and even if you were not a student, you felt at home with the crowd on the third floor. The next time I went, I wore my hair loose. "Aunt Irma, I left my ticket at home…" My stupidity earned me an expression of reprimand as she pushed me into the hall. She understood that her task had nothing to do with money or education. Her job was to expand the hall so it would take in any number of bruised little spirits that might come. When two years later, a regular student now, I showed up with an authentic ticket, it felt as if I had belonged to the Academy for ages.

My years at the Academy of Music were spent between attempts to conquer scholarship during the day, the euphoria of concerts in the evening, and, after I had begun my research, the ecstasy of religious services in the little secret prayer houses on Shabes and the Jewish holidays. The crowd on the third floor was like a circus troop, with its own dramas, loyalties and fights. I soon became friendly with the students and found my protectors among the older ones. At the beginning of each concert, we would peer down from the heights, scouring the parterre for familiar figures. At almost every concert, a distinctive grey mop of hair would appear somewhere in the middle of the hall. "Kroó is here," one of us would say. This meant that in the *New Music Journal*, the weekly radio program of musicologist György Kroó, we would hear his critique—garlands and flourishes of complicated sentences that we found enlightening and sincere without fail, even if we did not quite understand it. Then there was András Pernye, another musicologist and public figure. During the intermission, students and friends would gather around him in the aula. He would speak in a lively voice, with great intelligence and enthusiasm, his back to the wall, to support his paralyzed legs. He always stood at the same place, with a smile of undefeatable optimism on his smooth face. Until, one day, he committed suicide.

We were there when Sviatoslav Richter played, which he did often, stopping in Budapest on his way from the Soviet Union to the West. His concerts were not always announced in the monthly program. Still, by the time we arrived—normally an hour early, to be on the safe side—a row of policemen were protecting the entrance from a crowd ready to tear down the walls in order to get in. Somehow, in the end, everyone made it inside. We heard one of Yehudi Menuhin's last concerts with Hephzibah, at a time when he was in such a state that for each clean note, one had to suffer three others that were out of tune. For us on the third floor, it did not matter. When it was over, we kept applauding until the last lights were turned off and the guard came on stage, begging us to let him go home.

We went each time József Réti sang, whether it was Schubert or Bach; discussed the beautiful performances of the National Orchestra under the baton of János Ferencsik; held each other's hands in excitement during the unforgettable concerts of the Academy's student orchestra after months of agonizing rehearsals with Albert Simon, or Yumi, as everyone called him. We heard Maurizio Pollini's Schoenberg program, the Strasbourg Percussionists performing Varèse's *Ionisation*, Anja Silja singing Schoenberg's *Erwartung*, Zoltán Székely in Bartók's Violin Concerto, and the first full evening of works by György Kurtág.

Concerts were a *fête* and a ritual, and at the same time simple everyday events. No one understood this better than Annie Fischer. Whenever she stepped on stage, her delicate figure dressed in black, and put her hands on the keyboard, time would stand still. The magic lasted until the last notes faded, after which she stood up, bowed and left. It was one gesture, as simple as life itself. There was no need for raging applause from the third floor. It ended—we took our coats and went home. A feeling lingered in the evening air, a soundless music, sheltering beneath its wings the days until the next concert.

We, the students of the Academy, went about our lives as if we had been living in a fairytale country ruled by a just and benevolent king. I had never known a society so dedicated to an ideal and convinced of the truthfulness of its creed, while completely oblivious to any other reality. The blasphemous question, "How are you going to make a living doing this?"—which arose inevitably whenever I talked about my studies later in America—was never asked in those days, within the walls of the Academy. The scores of Bach, Beethoven, Schumann, Chopin, Brahms, Schoenberg, Berg, Bartók and the other "greats" were our Torah. They were the truth, and we were ready to give our lives for it.

At a certain moment during my studies, something went wrong. I began to have the disturbing feeling that I was living inside a giant bubble. In spite of our sheltered existence, or perhaps because of it, our ways of dealing with music began to impress me as an act of aggression. We would sit around the piano and analyze a sonata by Beethoven. But it was not analysis; it was a parade of mental antics and stunts of wit, which consisted of hurling clever-sounding remarks at each other in order to conclude with the composer's lofty praises: "Listen to this transition! And this modulation... What a genius!"

It was aggression, and it began to feel as though the music, on which such verbal excesses were spent, was also aggression. I had been drawn to classical music because it dared to *speak*. It was able to tell, in flames of passion, the story beyond the words. The joy of speaking was now being turned against itself. The whole enterprise began to resemble a chase of wild animals panting from exertion as they were running up the slope toward the peak of greatness. Where previously I had heard impassioned speech, I now felt the brutality of rhetoric. These symphonies, sonatas and nocturnes—they all wanted to "elicit an aesthetic response," to lure me into feeling. There was an imperative in every gesture: be sad or rejoice, but whichever it is, listen to *me*, for it is the great "I" that speaks.

When art is born from gestures of emotion—of longing and love—as in classical music, the performer must be forever on guard against perfection. The gestures of lovers, like those of music, are real as long as they are not planned. Music: an arm stretched out in longing—an arm thrown forward which, obeying the passion inside, is grotesquely exaggerated yet beautiful. True passion is unaware of its power, and the elegance of its gestures is born from obliviousness to form. But when lovers stretch their arms merely out of habit, when they become virtuosos in their motions, which are now perfect and final, the gesture will not need them anymore, but will take on a life of its own.

I became apprehensive about the myriads of empty gestures, even in some of the best concerts, displaying a sense of know-it-all and a desire to please and conquer. I remembered vaguely that music was supposed to be something else altogether. But my uncle Charles was far away, and the reservoir of grand emotions inside me used up.

I longed for sounds that spoke tentatively—not of grand emotions, but of the silence beneath them. I dreamt of music where instead of an "I" telling a story, there would be merely voices hovering in the air. I often heard such compositions in my dreams, but I never notated them. I could not reconcile the delicate sounds of these dream-pieces with the reality of performance: the sight of musicians on stage, their professionalism, pretentious gestures, smiles and cues, and above all the wheezing and coughing of the public nailed to their chairs. In my dream, there were no performers and no audience. We were simply *there*, the people and the sounds, as if by chance. Nobody made the music and nobody received it. A dream poured over us, and we wove ourselves in and out of it—the sounds and us.

I dreamt of music that flows like spring, shimmers and rustles like life. The days collide and bounce back, leave traces—trails of threads coiling themselves into fluffy knots, yarns weaving the fabric of their tales. No one plans and no one commands—it happens.

In my imaginary compositions, I wanted to tell a story the way I would do many years later, reading folk tales to my son. He would not allow me to explain the difficult words. "Don't tell it to *me*, just tell it." He stares into space and I look at the page. Devoid of will and intention, I release the sounds of the letters. We travel on the wings of words into the unknown, away from ourselves. Light years separate us from the characters in the story. I cannot imagine what is going through his little mind as he listens to these words, half of which he does not understand. He cannot know what the story means to me. Our parallel distances—the vast expanses between the story, him and me—connect us. In the blossoming vacant space, our mind-waves spin their spiral trajectories. We are shaken by the ever widening expanse, the breadth of nothing, which separates us and fills our hearts with hope and despair—the mysterious silence between the lines, the opacity of our lives.

The evening's radiant, fugitive time! Next year, next week, already the next day, our distances will be different. Evening after evening, we accumulate the mysteries of existence, which are swallowed by darkness the moment the story ends.

Morton Feldman writes: "What concerns me is that condition in music where aural dimension is obliterated. What do I mean by this? The obliteration of the aural plane doesn't mean the music should be inaudible—though my own music may sometimes seem to suggest this. Offhand I think of the Schubert *Fantasie in F Minor*. The weight of the melody here is such that you can't place where it is, or what it's coming from. There are not many experiences of this kind in music, but a perfect example of what I mean can be found in Rembrandt's self-portrait in the Frick. Not only is it impossible for us to comprehend how this painting was made; we cannot even fix where it exists in relation to our vision."

As I descended deeper in the world of traditional Jewish communities, I began to understand that it was not the notes that compelled me, but the whole: their lives—a life that *was* music. The sounds of the prayer hall were coarse, chaotic and ruffled, arbitrary and unplanned. They evoked in me the mystery of existence. In their well of ever deepening memory, a radiant and incomprehensible essence shone and around it formed layers of silence and mist, hesitancy, ambiguity and stumbling. In these sounds I believed I had found everything I had missed in classical music. In those days, I could not yet see the system of roots that lies under the surface and connects all music.

In a traditional *shul*, the service seems to go on forever, as though it never wants to end. The final mourner's *Kaddish* is followed by another, and yet another, each preceded by a psalm. This goes on as long as there are people who need to recite the *Kaddish* for a deceased family member. There is no final chord, no dramatic finale or resolution. The chanting continues, fading slowly into the noise of conversation, the squeaking of chairs and the shuffling of feet. As though the lulling melodies of prayer did not stop, but merely retreated for a while behind the curtain of noise of everyday life—until the next service.

I sometimes asked a member of the congregation to translate the text of a prayer for me. I remember the same scene repeating itself: the man pauses for a moment, stares at the Hebrew letters, and begins to hum a melody. The humming continues for a while, then, suddenly, he raises his head and looks at me to check whether I am ready. At that moment—the moment he looks up—he stops humming. Silence cuts the air. Then he begins to translate in a neutral voice, and I know that I won't learn anything that really matters. As long as he was praying, the meaning of the words emanated from the melody. Now, there is only a string of words—concrete, dry and objective.

It was the same with all of them—Gärtner, Roth and the others: first humming, then silence, and, finally, words without music. They were translating from a language and an existence in which *music and words are one.* They were translating a culture for which the meaning of words is *within the music*, into the language of a culture in which music and words had separated and become eternally alien to one another.

When people in *shul* sang coarsely and out of pitch, it was beautiful. When they sang proper melodies in a pleasing voice, it was empty and boring. But not always— it depended on whom you listened to. When they spoke, it sounded like a melody. When they gestured with their hands and swayed with their bodies, it was music. But when they prayed, it was melody and gesture and motion, the motion of the mind and the heart; it was ecstasy and argument, story and journey. With them, music, motion, words, thoughts and feelings melted together, and let go of their boundaries.

Why is it that the most beautiful melody is not a melody at all? What is it, then? Is it the sigh of the dead from behind the wall? The shimmer behind the curtain? *The taste of river?*

Emmanuel nodded: "I know what you mean. But you haven't seen anything yet. Come tomorrow at quarter to seven." I went with him to that secret prayer house on the second floor at the end of a long courtyard. It was then that I heard, for the first time, how a traditional Eastern European Jewish service might have sounded before the war. On that winter morning, it seemed transparent. My heart was filled with longing. I felt everything and could explain nothing. The heat wave that ran down my body would not tolerate words.

I remember—but not *when* it happened. On the time scale in my mind, I place it somewhere in 1976, although I am not sure. There was still snow on the ground—or was it snowing? Was it before I met Gärtner? Was it during my sessions with Roth? It could have been at any junction in my story.

Sometimes, it seems as if this encounter was not the first. The sound of their murmuring with no source and no aim, no beginning and no end has been in my ears since before I was born. It is the cloud that shelters my father's inability to sing. It is the resonance of the sobbing of my grandmother, the rhythm of the movements of my mother as she places the disinfected syringe into its metal container before going to sleep in the evenings, the whisper in the opening measures of Mendelssohn's violin concerto, the protective mist around me when I pass the police station on my way from synagogue to synagogue with the tape recorder around my shoulder.

Still, whenever I recall the noise of that prayer house, it always strikes me as fresh, as if I were hearing it for the first time.

In that prayer house, across the park, on the second floor at the end of the courtyard, was a man in a brown jacket. During prayer, he stood near me, on the other side of the curtain in the men's section, his back to me, facing the windows. He always wore the same jacket. I do not remember his face. Perhaps I never saw it from up close, since he was often late and left early, and stood with his back to me. He walked with a limp and had hearing problems, yet he was energetic and did not seem at all miserable. He moved fast, which was difficult to comprehend considering his lame foot. Whenever he entered and left the room, a current of air lingered behind him.

This man prayed for himself, in a muted and tired, monotone voice. His expression—or rather, lack of expression—and the swaying motion of his body stayed the same regardless of the holiday, the weather and the text; nothing mattered. He was not exactly speaking, but certainly not singing. His voice sounded like air in a thin reed; it had no color, depth or coherence. He had no sense of pitch; in his whispering *glissandi* there was no way of telling a major from a minor third or a minor third from an out-of-tune major second.

At first, I thought he must pray merely out of habit. He seemed to have no stake in it. He sang as though he were detached from his voice, sending it ahead to do the job while he waited patiently in the rear. "He is special," said Emmanuel. "He came from a village nobody heard of, in the middle of nowhere, and did not have much education. But he is terribly sharp and makes the best out of every situation. He is extremely popular in this community; we like him very much and would do anything for him. When you get to know him better, you will realize that nobody understands prayer more deeply than he does. He's in the heavens when he prays. He's completely unconscious. But most importantly, he's a good man."

I did not attend services regularly in that *shul*, but I went whenever I needed to be reminded of the *sound*. When I was there, I listened to the prayer of the man in the brown jacket—I had no choice, since he was standing next to me. The sound inside the prayer house seemed to be in constant transfiguration. Each time, it made a different impression on me; sometimes it was galvanizing, sometimes relaxing, one day mystical, another day dull. But an essence, which I could not name, remained constant.

One day, I realized I was not hearing the voice of the man in the brown jacket. More precisely, I was hearing it, but it no longer seemed to be his. It was simply *a voice*. A voice dismembered and detached, the voice of words, belonging to nothing but itself. It was part of the space, like the wooden column at the end of my bench or the light beam that poured in from behind the trees through the window. It contained everything that one could feel and imagine, and yet was distant—the voice of nowhere. I had never heard singing so inspired, a voice so beautiful and pure.

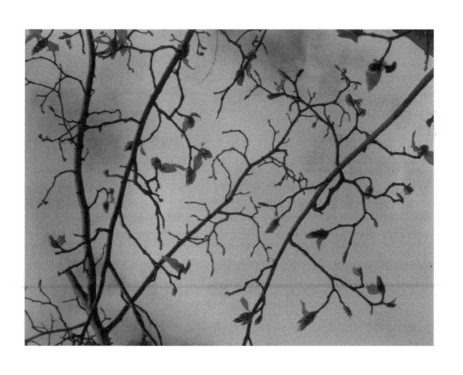

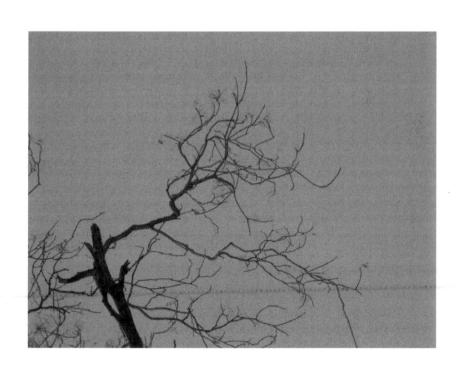

Serenity

"A man enters and leaves the world naked. And it is only naked—or nearly so—that he can enter and leave the wilderness. If he walks, that is; and if he doesn't walk it can hardly be said that he has entered. He can bring only what he can carry—the little that it takes to replace for a few hours or a few days an animal's fur and teeth and claws and functioning instincts. [...] The man who walks in the wilderness [...] immerses himself in what he is not. It is a kind of death."

(Wendell Berry, "An Entrance to the Woods")

It was during the summer of 1977 that I began my research in earnest. It took me a year of wandering from *shul* to *shul* to muster the courage to approach Gärtner, the first *baltfile* I worked with independently. That summer, I threw myself into my work. It is a mystery to me how I had the energy and collectedness to accomplish so much in such a short time. The recording sessions with Gärtner, Roth and the others kept me busy for most of the week.

Within less than two months, we had produced a sizable collection with full liturgies of the Shabes service and a respectable number of melodies for the High Holidays. At the beginning, Peter and I worked together, but after a while I preferred to be alone during the recording sessions. On Shabes, I attended services in order to familiarize myself with the customs of the different communities. I traveled to Sátoraljaújhely and documented the ritual of Hassidim from the United States who came to pray at the grave of *rebbe* Teitelbaum. I continued recording and visiting new prayer houses throughout 1977, and at the end of the year Peter and I made our first recording trip to Prague.

The following year, my recording sessions became less frequent, and after a last meeting with Roth in August 1978, I completely withdrew from recording for more than a year. I resumed fieldwork in the fall of 1979, in a state of panic, knowing I was about to emigrate. From then on until the end of 1980, my energy was fueled by the fear of being forever cut off from these voices that had grown in me like roots into soil.

On the surface, my retreat had a simple reason: in the spring of 1978, Peter and I got married and left the city. Our university scholarship, combined with the money we earned as part-time assistants at the Institute for Musicology, was not enough to rent an apartment. We settled in my parents' summerhouse—a tiny wooden cottage assembled from prefabricated wooden plates, hidden in the wilderness of the forest in the hills of Buda. The thin walls of the house defied all attempts to contain the little warm air given off by our electric heater, and in the winter we were literally freezing. Coming home from the city meant taking the subway to Moscow Square, a main traffic intersection in Buda, continue our travel by changing buses twice, then, after getting off at an abandoned station, walking a mile and a half along the open mountain ridge in scorching sun or raging wind, and, finally, climbing down an open stairway of a hundred and twenty-four slippery stone steps. Whether it was the layers of blankets in the winter or the euphoric beauty of the summer forest, it took determination to set out to town for a recording session or for anything else.

That wooden cottage in the hills became a shelter for my troubled mind. Far from the city, surrounded by the silence of the forest, I could listen to the melodies of the prayers without the emotional torrent they would unleash in me during services and recording sessions. For the first time, I was alone with the voices. It seemed that, finally, I was speaking with *them*—no longer involved with their faith, fear, social standing, misery and embarrassment. Nor with my shame, though it was overwhelming: the shame I felt about my privileged life on the one hand, and my inadequate Jewish background on the other. All this fell through the sieve. What mattered was what the notes were able to hold: the real shame, doubt, misery and hope that existed for the soul alone, and that had nothing to do with appearance, self-defense or phobia.

At recording sessions, the air was always thick with untold stories, unasked questions and embarrassed silences. Sometimes they clarified a point or recounted episodes from the past, but not a word was uttered about the most important thing. Now I realized that they had been talking to me all along, narrating stories in the most precise language: music.

But I did not speak the language of their melodies. Like a wanderer in the wilderness, the more I listened, the more lost and defenseless I felt. The reels of the tape recorder were turning with the sound-signs carved into the brown strips, continually flaking away, and I became confused, unable to imagine how these melodies were created, how they cohered into a musical system and what the meaning of the whole thing was supposed to be. I grappled with the realization of how alien these sounds really were. But I continued to encounter them, crossing vast terrains of multiple degrees of self-denial and estrangement. I no longer asked whether my efforts would be rewarded by a discovery presentable in the form of a scholarly argument. A wild inner force drove me. I listened, transcribed and created theories, which I almost instantly discarded, and kept listening, with a broken heart, exasperated, annoyed, and passionate to the point of madness.

In my nightmares, I saw yellowish-brown roads expanding over endlessly monotonous fields. Strings of caravans etched their traces into the surface, releasing particles of dust, which rose continually like smoke from a stricken flame. In another dream, worn-out people were wandering aimlessly through a snowfield. This second dream, in particular, returned frequently—probably because of the snow that covered our house most of the winter. In the dream, it felt as if I had been looking down on the earth from great heights, my head frozen in the cold outer space from where I observed the vast, blazing, white terrain sprinkled with black dots that moved with an almost self-effacing sluggishness, until suddenly all movement stopped, the image froze, and an unearthly calm descended, as if after an explosion. I heard soft steps on a wooden floor and gentle whispers, which I identified, absurdly, as the soothing voices of my great-grandparents.

After I had listened to the prayers so many times that they no longer moved me, I began to scrutinize them with the cool mind of a scholar putting fragments under a microscope. What splendid material! It was full of bizarre solutions and surreal turns, full of references, allusions and hints—the ambiguous flickering of clusters of ideas. As if in a fuse, ideas sizzled and flared up, each opening onto an entire system of luminous mythology.

The potential of musical fantasy is inexhaustible; the colors and layers of the emotions embedded in it endless. What music expresses is always a matter of perception, and interpretations are bound to be subjective and somewhat imaginary. When I first heard these melodies, they aroused in me a feeling of burning intensity, ecstasy and transcendence. But when I listened to them on the tape in my forest seclusion, they seemed to hold much more. They disclosed an amazingly wide and colorful world of thoughts and emotions. They narrated not one thing or another, but life itself with all its incompatibilities and eclecticism. I still heard transcendence and spirituality, but behind the lofty emotions, as though behind the knitted fabric of a curtain, shimmered a kaleidoscope of colliding images: nightmares, anxieties and desperation, small worries and tormenting memories, indifference, anger, boredom and fear, separation and reunion, home, strangeness and resignation, self-irony and skepticism, playfulness and humor, negligence and superficiality, and here and there even a morsel of vulgarity.

On the tape, someone is praying. The first syllable is on one pitch, and the second is on another—it is simple. The man reads the text as it is written, first only with two notes—up and down—then a bit further up and a bit further down: three notes, then four. He goes on weaving the melody from these four notes; he lingers on one as if looking around, dozes off on another, squeezes the next, whispers and sobs, and finally glides down the whole gamut of notes.

It is only that these sounds are not "notes." "Singing is a way of communication," my vocal teacher would say. "The voice should be clear, the pitches precise, and the performance explicit—a statement projected toward the public."

But there is no statement in prayer. In prayer, you send the sound of the words, detached and liberated, towards the unknown that is nowhere and yet all around and inside you—everywhere within and around. Before you formed it in your throat, the voice had been already singing in your veins, in your unconscious gestures and hallucinations. It emerges from the reverberation of the sound of your rushing blood, the ringing in your ear, the jingle of the air trapped in the room—the memory of the reso-

nances in the prayer house. And the sound that dwells in your ear is a soft amalgam of pitches; it is timid, hesitant, indecisive and a little confused.

How different this is from the clear and structured melodies of the Neolog services! I can recall the grandiose closures, when the choir, for instance at the Rabbinical Seminary, after a pompous melodic curve, lands on a noble "amen." It is a moment of relief and security: we have arrived. We have positively and unquestionably arrived home, to our warm and welcoming nest, and it is good for us to be here—or so says this glorious amen.

The sounds on my tape come from another world. *Davenen* sets sail from the harbor of everyday reality. It floats, vibrating with the tension of unanswerable questions, myriads of muddled emotions, memories and forebodings are stirred up and pull and push like forces in a magnetic field. *Davenen* is an existence eternally in formation; it is a meadow where flowers wither and vanish, are reborn and bloom each fleeting second.

The space of *davenen* is like a point stretched to eternity—without a sense of duration. From this journey and this space, one cannot arrive home.

Davenen is always rushed. Its notes are continually running after urgent and unfinished business, worried to be left behind and miss something. As if our lives were wrestling and tussling with the waves in a rapid stream. When we reach the shore, we barely have time to breath before we are washed away again by the waves—the perpetually swaying and undulating inner and outer life.

Davenen is *flight*. Through capricious ascents and descents, volatile and mercurial curves and diagonals, it speeds through the undecipherable puzzle—toward that which is known to exist but cannot be attained. The notes of *davenen*, aware of this, are always tinged with anxiety and a suppressed but burning desire for the final note—for the never-was-never-will-be home.

(These notes—these little nothings! *They live*: they weep and laugh and play and think. They long for the unknown and they break your heart. Or get bored and doze off.)

Davenen had become my daily bread. I dreamt it and woke with it, wandered through it like through a forest. I was no longer hearing scales and modes and melody types, but multitudes of fantastic sonorous assemblages that continually broke to pieces and cohered again into new constellations, like leaves and trunks and blossoms and flowers cohere into forest.

When I first read Idelsohn's book, I did not dare question its authority. But it seemed to me now that his approach, and theories of Jewish music that preceded it, were naïve. They took a melody for a string of colored beads. They cut the string and sorted the beads—the notes—measuring the proportion of the colors, their placement, densities and patterns: green is more common than red, blue always comes after white, and so on.

But melodies are not strings of beads. They are fantastic paths of flights drawn on an imaginary map. A three-dimensional map in the air—a *space*: the prayer house. From all corners, you hear people praying, each in his own way. You are surrounded—literally, not just figuratively—by multitudes of melodies, a sonorous cloud of disorderly, ambiguous and unpolished voices; you are embraced by the tangled and tousled branches of the sound-forest. You feel the "many" around you as the voices pull in a thousand directions.

At the same time, parallel to this, forgotten melodies are awakened *within you*; regions, epochs, spirits and thoughts come forward demanding their voices. You are lonely within this monumental mass of sound that calls out to you—the real sounds in the hall and the sounds of your soul from within. But suddenly, the sense of loneliness breaks and you give yourself over to the joy of being led by the voices and allowed to walk their path. And the chaos of the voices becomes your shelter. You fly—a weightless feather in the tumultuous clouds, which carry you toward benevolent skies.

The sound-cloud, like the scenery of a fairytale, brings about the most fantastic apparitions in a constant transformation: seagulls circle above your head and the sea gleams in purple, azure islands emerge in joyous streams, blazing clouds flow across the horizon of evanescence. In front of this perpetually boiling landscape, you stand still and tell your story. If you pray sincerely, you are able to listen without losing yourself. You put your foot firmly on the ground and let yourself be heard, obeying the demands of the sound-cloud, but at the same time resisting it.

For those who pray with compassion, every melody, even simple *davenen*, is a veritable composition. There are rules and styles and customs, and you are pulled in different directions by the voices from the crowd and your own memories. But this is only the framework within and against which you have to create *your* melody of this moment in your life and space—the melody that is born from a sense of existence that can never be repeated.

How did Roth say it? "The second important thing is *nisech*. When you pray for yourself, you may *daven* to whatever tune you wish. But when you pray for the community, when you lead the prayer, when you're a *baltfile*—or as we used to say it, a *shliach tsibbur*—you have to follow the *nisech*…" Each holiday, and within it, each prayer, and within that, each sentence and sometimes even each word, has its complex system of rules, its own *nusach*.

The *nusach* is the traditional path on the map and the prayer leader is the wanderer who follows it. He has to know the path for each prayer, which tonality, structure, motive and rhythm to begin with, how to continue and how to conclude, what voice, color and styles are allowed. He has to know the map, where it is possible to leave the habitual road, how to wander through unfamiliar terrains without getting lost in the forest. If he knows the path and the map and has fantasy and courage, he can take you to wondrous and magical places. He can lead you through secret paths that only he knows, show the way to tranquil lakes and islands, terrifying caves and chasms, clear springs and yellowed steppes. And even if for a moment it seems that we have lost the way, he takes us to our goal.

"When you are a *hazzn*—that is, a cantor—when you improvise, you don't need to stick to the *nisech*. But you have to know it, you have to have it in your head and be able to return to the simple form of the *nisech* at any moment, which is the most difficult thing. The essence is that even when I don't sing the *nisech*, I hear it in my head; the basic melody is always with me."

I was fortunate that life led me to Gärtner and Roth at almost the same time. For Gärtner, prayer meant the succession of miniature broken-up melodies. For Roth, it was the boundless, never-ending flow of notes. They sang the same *nusach*; their notes travelled on the same land and arrived at the same place. Gärtner was a man of the earth—he took you through a rugged landscape strewn with heavy rocks. Roth was a man of longing, who showed you rivers and the ocean.

"Let's imagine that in the communal knowledge of a people there are about ten, fifteen, or twenty basic melodies that never appear in their actual form, but are performed in a kind of free variation—they are improvised upon. They are always present in the background; they are in the air, so to speak, but appear always in different forms—we never hear the actual melody, only its variations."

(Bence Szabolcsi)

During my forest seclusion, I had little contact with my informants. Most of them had no phone and there was no telephone line in the cottage, either. I occasionally called those with private phones from my parents' home at the end of hurried visits, keeping the conversation to a minimum. After politely inquiring about their health, I would give a brief description of the forest, in the hope that it would be taken as an excuse for postponing my next visit.

I was not yet ready to see them. Their voices from the tapes in the forest—that was enough. This was what I had to understand first—the stories their voices told. The changing colors of the leaves, the fantastic calligraphy of the twisting branches, the dazzling colors of the butterflies swarming triumphantly over our terrace, the deafening clamor of the birds at dawn—all these were a mirror of the structures I heard on the tapes. Bent over transcriptions, the scholar in me was wandering in a music-wilderness whose underlying rules were transparent but whose reality was unpredictable and incredibly complex.

After months of work, it seemed that I might perhaps be ready to deal with the "whole." That is, until then I had cared only about the pitches (as much as the sounds on the tapes were pitches at all). But all along I had sensed that the secret of *davenen* lay elsewhere: in the *color* of the voices and in their *fluctuation*, the way they created something like time-waves, almost palpable in the air. These waves had impressed me alternately as precise—like measures and beats—and elusive.

I decided to transcribe one melody, rhythm and all, down to the smallest detail. After listening to it countless times, I began to feel a gently undulating pulse. I spent a whole afternoon trying to transcribe the melody to fit this pulse. The next day, while listening to the piece, I glanced at my transcription and saw that it had nothing to do with what

I was hearing. The beats were completely out of place. I transcribed it again according to the pulse I felt that day. The third day, the same thing happened: I heard a new pulse. In desperation, I turned on the metronome only to realize that the ticking clashed with the pulses I notated. The whole thing made no sense. It was exasperating. My jumbled transcriptions struggled to represent multiple clashing systems: pulsations juxtaposed onto each another and the motives, both set against the clicking of the metronome.

Yet when I listened to the piece, the effect was not in the least perplexing. The rhythm did not sound confused or even particularly complex; on the contrary, it seemed simple and natural. I put my analyses aside. I selected one of Roth's prayers and tried to sing it. After a few hours, I gave up. It was out of the question to keep up with his recitation, which was incredibly speedy and still calm like the waves of a river—a voice that resounded like a proclamation and at the same time was intimate.

"When you *daven*, you say the words, that's all you do, nothing else. Because *davenen* follows the text as you feel it, according to your rhythm and your voice. But the most important thing is not to add anything. You simply go with the words. Even if you don't feel anything, even then, you have to say it. You have to say it … for the sound of the words. Nothing but the words and their sound. In *davenen*, you do only what's essential."

I wondered what he meant by "the sound of the words … nothing but the words and their sound," and then by "because *davenen* follows the text *as you feel it, according to your rhythm and your voice*." Feel what? My rhythm? My voice?

I turned to one of Gärtner's prayers. His singing was melodious and structured, and after a few hours of practice I had gotten some results. It was not hard to remember his tunes, but my problem was to learn the style, to learn to sing like *them*, with their voices and rhythms, and through this exercise perhaps to understand what this is all about. I remembered how he said: "On Shabes, I would stand next to my father and copied him, I did exactly as he did, at least as much as I could, in my way, like children always do. He had his personal way in prayer, a unique and beautiful style. Till this day, I sing his melodies, or at least something similar, the way I remember them. Because they changed in the meantime … during the years I have been using them. The way I sing today—*this is my way, my personal nisech.*"

I decided to do the same. I would begin with memorizing his version of a prayer, imitating the notes, stops and breathing exactly as he did. I learned the basic melodic line quickly. Every morning, I would listen to the prayer and sing along with his voice from

the recording—it became a ritual. Once in a while, I would turn off the tape and try on my own. I would hear a stiff, strained voice. After weeks of work, the sounds I emitted were still somehow empty and dishonest.

⁓ᏋᎲᎧ⁓

One summer afternoon, I set out to town to run some errands. After traveling for an hour and a half through the dazzling panorama of the Buda hills, I arrived in Pest. Smelly vapor rose from the melting asphalt; the air was muggy, and the people sweaty and weary as they dragged themselves along streets that resounded with the noise of buses.

"I need to see *them*," I thought suddenly, "nothing more, just see them." I have not been to a service for several months. I made my way across Klauzál Square and down Dob Street to the complex of buildings that housed the Orthodox synagogue. Crossing the gate into the large L-shaped courtyard was like sliding out of life into a home, a dream—into the *shtetl*.

I passed Hanna's kosher restaurant and continued walking along the walls of the synagogue, until I reached the gate to Kazinczy Street. There was nowhere to sit, so I leaned against the wall, waiting for something to happen. A woman emerged from the kitchen; her face was familiar, but I could not remember her name. She noticed me.

"Good day. What happened to you that you haven't come to our services for such a long time? Is everything all right?"

"I'm waiting for Bence," I said.

"You must remember, he does not come before *minche*."

"I'll wait."

"No problem. Come, sit in the dining room."

"I'm fine, thank you."

I put my bag on the ground and remained standing near the gate. Silence enveloped me—a silence very different from what I had become used to in the forest: a self-contained quietude emerging from a landscape of withdrawal. Household noises—the clattering of kitchen utensils, muted conversations, a door slamming, a baby crying—filtered into the courtyard like thin air. I could have stood there forever.

I noticed two older men making their way along the wall of the synagogue; from the fragments of the words that reached me, I could tell they were engaged in a discussion. They were strolling slowly up and down without showing any sign of having noticed me.

I listened to their music. It was *music*: a complex and harmonious structuring of time. There was a rhythm to the movement of their bodies that highlighted the argument as they swayed back and forth. The rhythm broke up and reverberated in the flapping of their coats, complemented by the sound of their steps. There was a rhythm to the soundless narration of their hands and the movements of their heads and eyebrows; a rhythm to the intonation and changing color of their voices, the alternation of words and silences, in the way the wind carried these scattered fragments to me.

The movements and sounds cohered into polyphony, with tensions, collisions, incompatibilities and resolutions. It was like a medieval *hoquetus*, in which sparsely spaced fragmentary motives conversed with one another. It was like the beginning of the second movement of Bartók's *Fifth String Quartet*—where splinters of trills and *glissandi* exchange sigh messages across hollow space. It was like these, but free from any preconceived structure, involuntary and spontaneous.

I was spellbound. I remembered having witnessed similar scenes before, and the memory, though opaque, evoked a sense of refuge and security. Although the men spoke with their whole bodies, involving all their limbs in the argument, they did not seem agitated at all. It was as if what was taking place had been unfolding since time immemorial, under the rainbow vibration of the old covenant. Like paintings on which a thin layer of yellowish paint gives the effect of light coming from a great depth, an air of gentleness emanated from these men and at the same time covered them.

I waited for them to leave. I looked at my watch. In half an hour, it would be time for *mincha*. I picked up my bag and followed them out into the street.

I went home and spread the enormous sheets of my ever-expanding maze of analysis out before me. But suddenly, the whole enterprise seemed pointless. The short conversation in the courtyard had revealed more about music than all my analytical exercises. The lesson was simple: prayer is like life. A melody is life. And life: multiple pulsations and rhythms going on at the same time. Fragments of sounds, gestures and rhythms, connecting and clashing, emerging and fading, congealing and breaking off—each separate yet determined by the other. It is impossible to systematize. We walk, breathe or hum a melody, each with their unique rhythm, and combine them effortlessly into one whole. When we speak, we create complex rhythmic textures composed of the combination of the changing sonorities and lengths of syllables, breathing, accents, intonation and silences.

Music does not evolve according to a scheme. Music transcends our intelligent theories, which it kneads into its eternal depth. Music is ocean: with one gentle caress, it swallows up our ambitious and clever systems.

My forest seclusion was interrupted by a major project—a recording of Gregorian chant with the choir I had joined years before. The recording sessions took place in a church in a village not far from Budapest. The village was charming and the church was one of the most beautiful medieval structures in the region. To avoid the noise of the nearby highway, the sessions were held at night. We left Budapest in the evening and returned before dawn. In keeping with Catholic tradition, men and women sang separately—while one group recorded inside, the others could relax or chat in the nearby public school that the village had generously offered us for the time of the recording.

One session in particular stands out in my memory: the recording of a magnificent Responsory. We had been rehearsing the piece for almost a year; it had been especially difficult to memorize the florid free-rhythm ornaments and to create a unified color in our voices throughout a range of more than an octave. We start recording. We sing the piece from beginning to end—perhaps we'll be lucky and get through it in one take. But we have to stop at the second line: somebody is lagging behind. We start again. The second time is better, but we are still not together and someone is out of pitch in the middle section. Pay attention to the intonation. Make your voice disappear in the voices of the others. Let's try again. Better. But the sound is still a little coarse and the consonants are not completely together. Clear your voices of all blemish! We need a crystal clean, healthy and perfect voice. It should sound like a cord that is at once brilliant and transparent, yet strong as steel—like the voice of angel, pulling us up to heaven. Let's try again. Don't stick out. Feel the energy of the people around you. Listen to their voices, blend in, breath together, concentrate…

We stretch our voices, our nerves to the limit of human ability—the heat waves of our concentration are almost palpable. And just when it seems we cannot bear the tension any longer, a miracle happens: we are together. But it is no ordinary togetherness. It feels as if the melody is pulling us, as if some higher power is guiding us over an abyss—a mixture of euphoria and terror impossible to explain to someone who has never experienced it. The voice is so powerful that it makes mistakes virtually impossible; yet you know that the slightest slip would destroy everything. It is close to what an acrobat might feel when walking the high-rope: one part of the mind is secure in the body's ingrown sense of balance, while the other trembles with the fear of death.

We sing the Responsory perfectly. The last note fades away and for a moment, we cannot move—the miracle lingers over us. Then, suddenly, we start making noise—coughing, laughing, shuffling—anything we can do to participate in the ecstatic celebration of our return to life.

We deserve a break. We leave the hall in high spirits, talking and joking. I embark on a walk on the lonely streets of the village in the starlit night. My steps lead me to the edge of a field. Sounds reach me on the gentle dawn breeze: the noise from a nearby bakery, the barking of a dog, the whistle of a lonely bird and the rumble of a truck on the highway. Suddenly, I notice the squeaking of a door of a tiny synagogue and perceive fragments of *davenen*, that hesitant and confused, untamed and uncoordinated, always a bit out-of-tune and muddy sound-amalgam—sound-clouds forming, sound-rains pouring, sound-waves clashing into sound-waves. An opaque sense of home emerges from the odor of the morning breeze.

No, this cannot be. *Shachris*, the morning prayer, does not start before seven. Except that in this village, the Jews… Actually, the Jews in this village have been…

I walk back to the church. The door is open and the men who have just finished rehearsing are filing out through the arched gate of the aisle. I see groups of women disappearing into the beams of yellow light that stream through the entrance. I am supposed to go inside. "I am supposed to go inside," I say aloud. I feel weak, overcome by an irrational fear. I am freezing, my teeth are chattering. I tell the director that I am sick and need to lie down. No problem, she understands; it is exhaustion. I find a place at the back of the bus, pull my coat over my head and fall asleep.

By the time I awake, we have already reached the city. I dimly recall that I have an errand in town. I decide not to go home to our forest cottage, but instead to rest for a few hours at my parents' place. The moment I put my head on the pillow I fall asleep, but I wake up a few minutes later, entirely alert and ready to start the day. It is six o'clock and I have to be there at seven. I still cannot recall where and what *there* is. I fall back into a deep sleep.

At half past eleven, I am in the courtyard of the Kazinczy Street synagogue. *Shachris* ended hours ago and *mincha* won't start for some time. I am alone in the courtyard. I try to open the door of the synagogue, but, as could be expected, it is locked. I stroll back and forth between the gates, then sit down on the stairs leading to Hanna's. I walk back to the synagogue and try the other entrance. I turn the knob. It opens.

I have never been on the first floor, in the men's section. It is strange to walk on these tiles, which until now I had seen only from above. Where would I sit if I were a man? How would I sing if this was not our century and I was not I?

At the back of the hall, prayer books are piled up on a table. In a daze, I cannot seem to remember why they are there and what they are for. I open them one by one. They are mostly without Hungarian translation and some have lengthy explanations in Yiddish, written in small, strange looking characters. I feel a sudden urge to read a Hebrew text as I did at the beginning, when I understood nothing.

Oh, my intelligence, my mind, my voice! Sure, my voice is capable of anything; it can change color like a chameleon. My mind can expand to digest any religion, ideology, aesthetic, and musical style that comes its way. Let it be silent now. I want to teach it to give things space *to be*. What if I did not want to understand everything? If I would just let it be—my pathetic voice that cannot pray. I want to suffer through a text from beginning to end, word by word, letter by letter. I need to return to the beginning: to hear the letters uttered by *my voice*, in the way only I can recite them, be it bad, mistaken, ridiculous, anything—the sound of the letters. Let the sounds do their work.

I search through the books. Although my knowledge of the prayers is minimal, there are few texts that contain nothing familiar. I want something that is completely unintelligible. I do not want to give my mind any hints, for it to begin figuring out the meaning like a crossword puzzle. After some searching, I find a *machzor* for *Shvies. Akdomus*, I think. I have a general idea of its message, but there is no chance I will understand this poem by the eleventh-century Rabbi Meir ben Yitzchak of Worms, written in terse, medieval Aramaic.

I take the *machzor* and look around for a place with enough light to read. The situation is absurd. I do not know what I would say if someone entered the synagogue. What am I doing here, a woman in the men's section, reading the text of *Akdomus* a week before *Tishebov*? But I am completely oblivious to the possibility of such a scenario. I sit down, open the *machzor* and begin to read. I read the text syllable by syllable, skipping none of its ninety lines and understanding almost nothing.

I am bewildered by the exotic sonority of the words as they resonate in my coarse, singing whispering voice like an ancient incantation. Nobody comes by. When I finish, I close the book and put it back exactly where I had found it. I step out into the courtyard, close the door and go home.

אַקְדָּמוּת מִלִּין, וְשָׁרָיוּת שׁוּתָא.

אַוְלָא שָׁקִילְנָא, הַרְמָן וּרְשׁוּתָא.

בְּבָבֵי תְּרֵי וּתְלָת, דְּאֶפְתַּח בְּנַקְשׁוּתָא.

בְּבָרֵי דְּבָרֵי וְטָרֵי, עֲדֵי לְקַשִּׁישׁוּתָא.

גְּבוּרָן עָלְמִין לֵיהּ, וְלָא סְפֵק פְּרִישׁוּתָא.

גְּוִיל אִלּוּ רְקִיעֵי, קְנֵי כָּל חוּרְשָׁתָא.

דְּיוֹ אִלּוּ יַמֵּי, וְכָל מֵי כְּנִישׁוּתָא.

דָּיְרֵי אַרְעָא סָפְרֵי, וְרָשְׁמֵי רַשְׁוָתָא...

א 'Akdomus milin, veshoroyus shuso

א 'Avlo shokilno, harmon urshuso.

ב Bevovey terey uselos, de'eftach benakshuso.

ב Bevorey devarey vetarey, 'adey lekashishuso.

ג Gevuron 'olmin leyah, velo sipek perishuso.

ג Gevil ilu reki'ey, keney kol churishoso,

ד Deyo ilu yamey, vechol mey chenishuso,

ד Doyrey 'ar'o sofrey, veroshmey rashvoso…

א In introduction to the Words, and Commencement of my speech,

א I begin by taking authorization and permission,

ב In two and three sections, I shall commence with trembling,

ב With permission from Him Who created everything and shields it till its
hoary age,

ג His is eternal strength that could not be described—

ג Even if the heavens were parchment, and the forests quills,

ד If all oceans were ink, as well as every gathered water,

ד If the earth's inhabitants were scribes and recorders of initials…

The Finger-Telescope's Story

The color of *shalashides* is white and gray. Every Shabes afternoon I went to the same study room where, week after week, a group of about twenty, mostly elderly men and women gathered for this ritual communal meal.

When I close my eyes, the colors and the lights of the room come back to me, and I am able to replay those hours to myself like a film. I hear the echoless, dampened conversations rise like hot air from the radiator, whispered sentences wilting into sighs of resignation. I see the winter sky stretched across the window like an enormous gray drapery. I remember the washbasin and the bucket at the entrance, the row of soda bottles, the greasy brilliance of the plastic table cover, and the patterned curtain behind the bench, which had been hung there to hide the crumbling wall. White paper plates, matching the number of chairs, contain a painstakingly egalitarian portion of two sardines each. A yellowish roll is placed on a napkin at the side of each plate. White plastic cups, metal-colored thermoses, and more paper plates filled with butter cookies, oranges and apples are arranged in the middle of the table.

The color of Shabes *shachris*, the morning prayer, is blue and gold. The sky, slowly detaching itself from the rising beam of red light, inundates the room, and the darkness of the benches is brushed away with a shimmering blue and the cozy yellow of the light bulbs. Shabes morning is ecstatic.

Shalashides, the third and last ritual meal on a Shabes afternoon, is like a simple farewell, casual and quiet, perhaps a bit even tired. The men tell jokes, discuss politics, and complain about the rabbinate. Some, holding their books, eyes fixed on the page, are immersed in study. Others are sitting quietly with an empty expression, thoughts wandering. A few boys and girls congregate in a corner, where one of the men is holding the weekly Torah lesson.

It begins almost unnoticeably: someone starts to leaf through a prayer book. He locates the pages with the texts traditionally sung during *shalashides*—a selection of *zmires*, poems composed for the various rituals of Shabes. He finds the poem first to be sung at the *shalashides* table, pushes back his chair and begins to sing. Some join in immediately, while others continue talking, reaching lazily for their prayer books and flipping the pages as if searching for the text, although they all know it by heart. A heavyset man has just finished telling an anecdote; he begins to sing with a forceful voice but stops after the first verse; apparently he has come to a realization that urgently needs to be shared with his neighbor.

After a few stanzas, almost everyone is singing—most of them casually, as if all this does not really matter. Meanwhile, an old man insists on reciting the text without melody, like an oration. At some point the singing becomes so relaxed that one can barely recognize the rhythm. Now the youths in the corner raise their heads from their books and step in with loud and precise voices. But the elders cannot bear their gaudiness for very long and pull the song back into its former, comforting sloppiness.

The last notes fade away, and there is a moment of silence. Perhaps someone will start another song, perhaps according to the traditional order of the *zmires*, perhaps not. The men rarely sing the entire *zmires* repertoire of *shalashides*. They are content with a few, and often even with a fragment of one song—it is enough to have a taste of the singing. After the songs, the natural noises of *shalashides* quickly return: the crumpling of plastic cups, the squeaking of chairs, and the murmur of conversation.

"It's time for *minche*," a voice cuts in. Although immersed in conversation, the *balt-file* looks up and moves away from his place at the table. On his way to the lectern, the book already open in his hand, he nevertheless finishes his story. Then he places the prayer book on the lectern, and, without waiting for silence, naturally and spontaneously as if he were merely continuing his story, begins to recite the prayer for the last ritual, the Shabes *mincha*: "*Ashrey…*"

It takes a few minutes for the chatter in the room to give way to *davenen*—a sound that is unified and melodious, spiritual. A few men stay behind at the table and begin to collect the paper plates, the soft voices of their conversation a counterpoint to the murmuring sound of the prayer. Outside, the clouds part and snow begins to fall—a sparkling mirage that seems to answer the gentle blur of sounds in the room.

I have the strange feeling that the *mincha* is a more casual ritual than the one that took place around the table a few minutes earlier. As if, after the playful clashes and dramas during the singing of the *zmires*, which had an air of theatricality, we have come back to our real home: *davenen.*

The task assigned to me by the Academy of Sciences was to collect Jewish folk songs. I was supposed to produce the *Critical Edition of Hungarian Jewish Songs*, similar to the famous *Corpus Musicae Popularis Hungaricae* presenting thousands of Hungarian folk songs—transcribed, annotated, catalogued, classified and analyzed. And indeed this was what I set out to do: I imagined becoming the scholar who would create, from the asphalt wilderness of Budapest, the Jewish parallel of Hungarian folk music.

For me, Hungarian peasant songs meant the peak of musical art. Their perfect and restrained form held immense emotional depth. I knew these songs mostly from recordings, and only once, at a scholarly conference, did I have the opportunity to hear the traditional performance of old-style Hungarian songs. I remember the three heavyset, middle-aged Hungarian peasant women who were already on stage by the time the conference participants gathered in the auditorium. They stood as if they had spent all their lives on the podium, calm and indifferent, and yet utterly displaced. They began to sing, without any preparation or cue. Their bodies and faces remained motionless throughout their performance of the many stanzas of the ballads. Their nonchalant, matter-of-fact voices were like hardened earth, and still everything about them was immediate and natural, and even the most elaborate ornaments flowed effortlessly from their mouths. They sang stanza after stanza the way one turns the pages of a book. As if they did not notice that the sorrow on each page weighed a hundred tons.

After hearing the singing at *shalashides*, I was left with a heart-rending feeling: I was ashamed that the Jews I encountered seemed unable to produce a musical performance that was as strong, restrained and yet expressive as that of these women. Strangely, while among them, I was not at all bothered by their sloppiness—in fact, I even enjoyed it. But after I had arrived home and replayed the performance in my mind, I felt embarrassed.

Jewish prayer yearns for the unattainable and therefore cannot be song-like; it must be prose—an open-ended form, I thought. But when I looked at the prayer melodies more closely, I saw that they were composed of a sequence of pairs of lines and pairs of pairs—it would take only a slight sharpening of rhythm to turn them into song. Like a secret emblem, songs were woven into the fabric of *davenen* and *nusach*. Floating in the waves of *davenen*, minuscule song-like formations constantly surfaced and sank back into the waves. They were like secret signs, enigmatic potentialities and suggestions. They were embryos waiting to be born.

In the prayer houses where I used to attend services, only a few texts were performed as songs; for instance *Lecho doidi*, *El odain*, parts of the *Hallel*, and some verses from the High Holiday services. The melody of these songs was often reminiscent of the *nusach*, as if the *baltfile* had merely solidified the rhythm of the *nusach* melody he had just been singing. But it also happened that the song was completely alien: there were Ukrainian, Russian, Rumanian, Polish and Hungarian folksongs; waltzes, tangos, marches, mazurkas; operetta and cabaret melodies. The *baltfile* might surprise us with an out-of-place tune, even for the text of the noblest prayer. True, such outlandish melodies were rare, but there was always the possibility for one of them to pop up from the river of *davenen*.

I remember when, during a recording session with Gärtner, we came to the text *Hallelu* in the *Hallel*, somewhere in the middle of the prayer. He suddenly stopped singing and closed the prayer book: "That's all … that is the *nisech*. The rest we can skip. When you come to this point, from here until the end of *Hallel*, you sing songs, a different one for each section of the text, one song after another. There are a few instances where you should go back to the *nisech*, like at the end, but that's nothing special. When you have a text that needs a song, you can sing whichever tune you like, whatever comes to mind. And if you can't think of any, then continue with the *nisech*."

During service, when the *baltfile* began to sing, some of the men joined in energetically, as if they had been waiting for this moment. But their enthusiasm did not last

long. Like at *shalashides*, they had no patience to continue with the orderly rhythm and disciplined uniformity of stanzas and soon slipped back to the soothing atmosphere of *davenen*. As if they were sending a message to the *baltfile*: "We know it's customary to sing these verses to proper tunes, and we know you do, too, and since we all know that we all know, let's go back to *davenen*." For the most part, the *baltfile* was also uncertain. He would begin a song and sing the first line properly. But by the second line, his rhythm would loosen and the melody would collapse into something close to the style of *nusach* and *davenen*. Then, at the last line, as if suddenly remembering that he was supposed to sing a song, he would pick up the proper melody and rhythm of the song, only to drop it immediately: why bother—the stanza is about to end anyway.

Whenever, during my lonely hours in the forest, I began to analyze the songs, I almost immediately abandoned my work—apprehensive, as if walking on the wrong path. Still, I could never shake off the feeling that something obvious and simple was hidden from me. It could not be that the songs did not matter. Perhaps the songs had their own spiritual world—outside of prayer, another dimension that was more tangible and close to earth, separated from everyday life only by a thin veil. Sometimes I felt that by allowing myself to become lost in *davenen* and *nusach*, I was turning away from an essence. But they drove me mad, these songs—I could not make sense of them! It is true: there were many beautiful pieces. But I was bewildered by the sloppiness of the performance, and the eclecticism of the whole.

⚜

I suddenly remembered a conversation during our visit to Prague in 1977. Talking to Victor Feuerlicht, the *baltfile* of the Altneueschul, I gathered my courage and asked him: "Why is it that we Jews don't sing together? Why do we have such a bizarre collection of melodies—even within the ritual? Shouldn't we care more about songs—what we sing and how?"

Feuerlicht did not seem in the least offended. He smiled, and began to explain.

"The songs … the songs are not necessary for the prayer. But at the same time, they are very important to … how shall I say … to this whole thing. Because it is not that you sing a song. No, it's not so simple. You need fantasy. To compose a song is real art, and to understand and sing it … you need fantasy. And you need an audience, a special community for that."

"The songs … there are plenty of them … of all sorts. In my time, before the war—I was a Talmud student at Hanusfalva between 1936 and 1938—the songs kept coming from the *chazunim* and the poets. They came from Poland and Romania, because our *rebbe* had many followers, many Hassids, all over the world, and among them were many musicians, singers and composers—talented people. They would work on their compositions all year round. During the summer, before the High Holidays, they submitted two or three of their best songs for the *rebbe* to choose from. They sent them on paper. At the court of the *rebbe*, there were musicians who could read the notes and would play the melody for him on the violin. If, after hearing a song, the *rebbe* said: 'Yes, that's good,' we invited the composer so that he could sing the song for the *rebbe* and teach us—we were a small choir of about twenty, twenty-four boys. We learned the songs and sang them at the High Holidays, at *Sikes, Simhes Tayri*, Chanuka, Purim— those occasions when you need songs in the prayer, and we sang them also during the High Holidays and on Shabes at the *rebbe*'s table."

"With the help of the composer, we matched the text to the melody. The text came from the prayer book; it was fixed and its syllables and phrases often did not match the number of notes and the phrases in the melody that the *rebbe* had chosen for the text. It took quite some work to figure out how to apply the melody to that text. Because this was not important to the *rebbe*: he did not care whether the syllables matched the notes. He cared only for … the atmosphere ... how shall I say… the meaning … the soul in the text and in the melody. He listened attentively when the tune was played, contemplating it. He considered carefully, sometimes for a long time, which text was hidden in the melody. And when he finally found it … when he suddenly understood that, for example, a certain melody expressed the essence of the poem *Sholaim aleichem,* he would tell us, and that tune would serve as the melody for the *Sholaym alechem* the following year. It was the same with other songs. Each one found its text, according to the thought of the *rebbe*, and throughout the year, whenever that text came up in the liturgy, that is what we used. There were twenty-something new songs each year."

"It was a great thing, this summer preparation of the songs. There were beautiful melodies in those days, veritable compositions with original ideas and imagination. We lived with these songs; the composer taught them with their precise rhythms, accents and dynamics: when to be soft and when to sing in full voice, when to bring out the beat, speed up and so on, all the details. To tell you the truth, sometimes I felt that it was a waste, all this careful preparation, because when the congregation joined in, there was always a mass of sound pulling us in all directions and often the entire thing fell apart. But we had to lead them. We had to give them an idea of where this music was going and what was its essence … its effect, its feeling. It was all very important—to bring out the essence of the melody … its soul, so to speak. At the same time, that was good … it was fine for the congregation to do it as it felt … that was also part of it. That was the beauty of it, that everyone took it somewhere else."

"Sometimes a song survived for several years. It became such a hit that neither the *rebbe* nor the community wanted to change it. Nothing better came along. And as long as no better melody came, we stuck to the one from the previous year, which we were already used to. For instance, the *Sholaim aleichem* we have just recorded was a very successful composition. The *rebbe* had many followers, thousands came for the High Holidays, and everyone wanted to learn the *rebbe's Sholaim aleichem*, so that they could take it home and sing it with their family. It was extremely popular in those days and the people praised the composer who put it together. Were it not for the war, this *Sholaim aleichem* would have survived until our days. With me… With me, it survived."

"It also happened that a melody had several texts. One rabbi thought it suited this text; another thought it suited that text. People moved from place to place and took the songs with them, and sometimes the same melody went around with different texts. For instance, the one I just sang to the text *Pischi li sharey tsedek* from the *Hallel* was the melody for *Sholaim aleichem* in other circles. In fact, it was the rabbi's favorite *Sholaym alechem* in 1937, if I am not mistaken."

"Songs were especially important during the High Holidays. We never changed the *nisech*, of course; it remained the same traditional melody year after year, because the *nisech* is the core. We needed songs only for certain poems or certain lines within the prayers. During the High Holidays, the rabbi served as the *baltfile*; he sang the *misef* and the *nile*, and often parts of the *shachris*. That's why we needed songs—in order to give the *baltfile* an opportunity to rest. He prayed with such devotion! And these holidays lasted for the entire day, and he prayed with concentration … all day long … it was exhausting. He knew that he could count on us, on the choir, that when we were singing, he could rest. Otherwise, you wouldn't need songs … in principle. It would be enough to say the text with the *nisech*. But the songs helped the *baltfile*."

"Every person and every community and every era has its style. In my village, Huszt, where I was born, the people wept when the *hazzn* began the *Hineni heoni*. You won't believe it, but the men standing around me… I was still a child, but I remember clearly: the men around me wept with real tears. There was nothing to that melody, a simple *nisech*, anyone could do it, and still they wept. Today, this is unimaginable. Indeed, what do people have to weep about? With their apartments, cars, life insurances, and trips to Paris—now tell me, what is there to cry about? It is the same with the songs. The way these young neo-religious sing … on the cassettes I am getting from Israel! Like the soldiers' choir at the ceremony for the Great October Revolution! But let them do as they wish. This is their life … and we have … something else. Whatever that is … we have … you sing what you have."

When I first heard Feuerlicht speak of the songs, I thought his story was irrelevant to my question; it seemed to relate to the custom of a specific community. But recalling our conversation after months of perplexing analyses in the forest, it struck me as fundamental. I hastened to jot down whatever I remembered and decided to record his explanation on my next visit to Prague. As I was making notes in the margin of my field diary, I glanced at the list of pieces we recorded, and it suddenly dawned on me that we collected almost exclusively songs.

I recalled how, on that first visit, I felt disoriented, not knowing if it made sense to spend only a few days with a certain community. In Budapest, I lived in a sensation of endless time: the weekly ritual of recording sessions. Jewish services are long and complex, and it is unlikely that one could ever record all the melodies. Even if we were to complete all the holidays, there would always be another topic for yet another session: a different version of a particular prayer, a melodic insertion for a minor holiday or some other detail missed earlier. The recording sessions, which were the pretext for our meetings and the token of our friendship, had to continue.

On the day Peter and I arrived in Prague—we had chosen a Friday, so that we would be able to meet people immediately at the synagogue during the evening service—I spent the afternoon in the *Zimmer* we were renting in an old lady's apartment. Peter was eager to explore the city, but I decided to stay home. I paced up and down, thinking about how to begin, until I looked out the window and realized that the afternoon—and with it my first day in Prague—was gone. Staring at the darkness for a long time, I gradually reconciled myself to the thought of a project altogether different from what I had been doing so far.

It would have been unreasonable to attempt the recording of full services during a weeklong visit. My friendships, too, would have to be of an entirely different sort. I would be in Prague for only a few days, then leave for who knows how long. Perhaps I would come back next year, perhaps never. I felt as if I were slipping into another reality: a reality of the here and now, of things that emerge and fade away instantaneously, a world where one needed the ability to live through *an essence within a moment*.

The Friday evening service at the Altneuschul synagogue was similar to what I knew from Budapest, only even more haphazard. In the middle of the prayers, a wave of fatigue came over me. I could barely hold myself up, and was waiting for the service to end.

You know that prayer has a set time and that the service will end, and that it is you who sets its beginning and end. And yet, as you begin to pray, it seems as if you were not beginning anything at all. It is as if you were merely plunging into a state of being that had continually been happening around and within you—a state of being beyond time.

The sensation of timelessness is interrupted by the song. It stops the flow of *davenen*. Its memory remains; you still feel the caress of the waves on your skin, its pulsation and rhythm are in your ears, but you are already at another place. You stepped outside. Where to? Where does one step out to from eternity (*davenen*), which is inside finitude (the timeframe of the service), which is within what feels eternal but is actually finite (one's life)? Stepping out from time's continual flow, the song frames *the moment*.

During the service, oblivious to the prayer, I was weaving thoughts about time. I woke up from my half-dream when I saw the congregants filing out of the synagogue. A simple song accompanied their procession to the adjacent room for the *Kiddush*. I had never heard this song. I later learned that it was the unique custom of this community to keep singing that particular melody until all the congregants had left the prayer hall and taken their place around the *Kiddush* table. This otherwise commonplace song moved me more than anything in the service. It expressed something the recitation of prayer could not: a feeling of *here and now*.

In those days, Prague was in bad shape; it looked even worse than Budapest. After the defeat of the Dubček revolution, the city took on an air of apprehension and mourning, people were lethargic, and the buildings, mirroring the spirit of their inhabitants, were neglected. The walls were covered with layers of soot and the plaster decorations were crumbling. Like Budapest, this city, beautiful in its sluggishness, was a labyrinth of unasked questions; it compelled you to try to decipher what was not immediately apparent. Its atmosphere awakened in me a feeling of solace—a feeling much deeper than what the renovated Prague of today offers its tourists. Before the renovation, Prague did not cater to the casual passerby; the visitor needed imagination to recognize its beauty.

I loved to walk around the streets and engage in spontaneous conversations about Nietzsche with street vendors—who, as it turned out, were jobless philosophy professors. I enjoyed the music of the sweet lady's voice that accompanied the opening and closing of the subway doors. I photographed and collected details with my mind and eyes—details I would probably never see again—while all the time I was thinking about Jewish songs.

One day, as I was traveling on the subway, the image of the Hungarian peasant women from the conference came to my mind. I remembered how strong they had seemed to me as they held themselves motionless and erect. These women knew the evil of the world; they knew what forces they had to withstand in order to survive. Their songs were rocks, enduring and stable against the deluge. But those old Jews I met in Budapest and Prague did not trust anything that was part of their material existence. For them, the only stable ground was an imaginary path in the air, a flight leading through clouds and sky: the longing for the unknown—*davenen*. Songs needed all their strength to stand firm against the stream of *davenen*. The island—the song—is always afraid of the waves. There is always rushing water around us, and the rocks melt away before your eyes.

Yes, I told myself, the recitation holds the one and only thing that matters: longing for the *beyond*. And exactly for this reason—I suddenly understood—Jews needed songs. Songs are also a foundation, even though they crumble and collapse and submerge in the cascades of *davenen*. Songs are not eternity. They are the anything of the here and now.

Songs are anything that life's simple moments may bring. They are the awakening from the dream of *davenen*—the awakening to the world—or the opposite—the descent into an even deeper dream. Songs are windows to the outside and also to things inside, to visions, myths and dreams.

The songs bravely face whatever happens to come along: czardas, mazurka, tango, or march—sentimental or insipid, nostalgic or vulgar. They are the garbage and the waste, the forbidden and the appalling—a heterogeneous mass, a collage of haphazardly gathered, eclectic fragments. Heterogeneity is courage. It is the daring acceptance of *anything that comes*. It is the shameless admittance of one's smallness. Songs: the trash heap of days.

Or else: a song opens a window onto the depth of the imagination. It might be a little nothing, a snapshot, a gesture, or a sophisticated and complex composition. But form is only surface. Climbing inside the world within its outer shell, one descends into layers of darkness and unaccounted faith which neither the simplicity nor the complexity of form can account for. A song knows the sorrows, the stupidities, the joys and the silences of the real world, and also those of the beyond. It knows the absurdity of life and the absurdity of prayer, and it laughs at its own absurdity. It knows the luminosity of loneliness. Beneath the story of the song lies silence. And after its silence: a smile.

I wrote in my notebook:

The recitative (davenen, nusach):   river ... eternity ... the *kadosh* ...
The songs: islands ... the things of the world ...

The recitative: ... elimination of the "I," loneliness, longing for God ...
The songs: ... the presence of "we," the world, life ...

The prayer: ... the privilege of presence in a sensation of eternity ...
The song: ... grasping of the moment in eternally withdrawing time

Here is the song for one of the texts of the *zmires*—a simple blessing after the meal in couplet form: "Tsur misheloi ochalnu / borchu emunoi, / sovanu v'hoisarnu, / kidvar adoinoy ..."—"The Rock from Whose we have eaten! / Bless Him my faithful friends! / We have eaten our fill and left over / according to the word of God." This is how it goes:

"Tsur misheloi ochalnu":
a descending motive in minor mode

– contemplation;

"tsur misheloi ochalnu" (repeated):
fanfare-like variant of the same motive in major mode

– affirmation, proclamation;

"borchu emunoi":
a major triad that suddenly, as if doubting its optimism, reaches and, then, drops below the minor cadence

– question, hesitation, doubt;

"tsur misheloi ochalnu / borchu emunoi…"
(both verses repeated):
a new motive in major, in an entirely different style: jumpy and naïve with symmetrical rhythm, like a children's mocking song, a limerick

– playfulness, parody? self-irony?;

"sovanu v'hoisarnu":
ascending melody in low register in minor mode

– a raised finger that commands attention;

"kidvar adoinoy":
In this last melodic line, as if your eye glimpsed something unexpected and uncalled for, you recognize the elevating and solemn melody of the *Kol nidre*, the penitential prayer for Yom Kippur

– a shimmer of eternity, of the beyond.

This twenty-second long melody contains volumes of arguments and counterarguments: contemplation → proclamation → hesitation → self-irony → a raised finger → and finally: prayer, that is, eternity.

I had heard this song from the man sitting next to me at the *Kiddush* after the service at the eve of Shabes at the Altneuschul. He sang it casually, as if murmuring a story to himself, and I wished that he would never stop, so that I could listen to that strange little melody in his warm and gentle humming voice forever. When he finished, I asked him—as I could think of nothing better to ask—where the melody came from. "Are you the scholar from Hungary? I am Dr. László Mészáros. I heard of your visit to us… So happy to meet you!" From that moment until the end of the *Kiddush* and afterwards, during our walk, we did not stop talking. At one point, I asked him to explain the melody of *Tsur misheloi*. He looked surprised: "Explain the melody? What is there to explain?"

It took me many years to understand what he meant. But perhaps I had always understood it. Something inside me, something less intellectual and more perceptive—the mind of a child—had already grasped that a simple song is able of containing the universe. I knew what every child knows: that when we allow our fantasy to act, even a small and insignificant object like a toy or a pebble or a song becomes larger than what it seems to be. For the imagination, objects are vessels for the unknown—veils behind which lie things much deeper, dreamlike, and therefore infinitely more real.

On the seashore in Maine, after rehearsals, Charles and I would often play the game of the "finger-telescope." I knew this game from my childhood, having played it with the other children during summers at the healthcare workers' resort at Lake Balaton. We would curl our hands, so that the thumb and fingers formed a circle: this was the lens through which you could observe a scene. The landscape stretched from the mountains to the lake down to the fields: an endless blue canvas of sky, yellow sand with patches of dried-out shrubs, birds and lizards bathing in the sun, umbrellas on the beach, the ice-cream man, swimmers, children and sandcastles, sunburnt red roofs below the faraway mountain ridge and a serpentine road with cars, which seemed, from the distance, like sluggishly crawling bugs, the steamship in the harbor and sailboats, a toy shovel and sand bucket left on the ground. Closing your fingers, you zoomed in on part of the landscape. The eye of the telescope became smaller and smaller, you saw only a patch of vibrating sand until finally, through the minuscule tunnel, a tiny pebble appeared with a network of fine blue lines on its surface.

You look through the finger-telescope and study the universe in the lines on the pebble. The lines commemorate the earth's cataclysm that happened millions of years ago. They are like the veins on the back of your hand. They are signs of a dead language, or the map revealing the path to a hidden treasure. They are whatever you want them to be and have the fantasy to see. They are a song: a drop from the timeless, ever-changing river.

(Nowadays, when those first years of ethnographic work in Budapest and Prague and my analytical enterprises in the forest seem almost as remote as my childhood, I think of the songs as precious stones holding a secret that is meant to be felt without being fully disclosed. When I try to recall the moments a Jewish song moved me, what comes to mind are not the services or the *shalashides* gatherings, but the recording sessions. I understood then that songs are miniature stories and teachings. You are not an outsider if you don't join in. It is enough if you listen.

I would put the microphone on the table and witness the same scene repeat itself over and over again, regardless of who I was recording. He would be silent for a while, and then say: "This is how we used to sing it at my father's home." The melody was not particularly expressive or complicated. After all, it was only a song—a few notes. "That's all," he would say at the end, and we felt that nothing more needed to be added. During his singing, silence thickened around us. The vast melancholy of the sounds awakened our senses and filled our minds with a vague inkling of the past. He could barely remember what I would never be able to imagine: the life "before.")

Dr. Mészáros was a pediatrician and therefore very busy. When we met again in Prague, two years later—the meeting turned out to be our last before he died—he suggested that we record on New Year's Eve, his only free evening: "You must know that, first,

I have no voice, and second, I don't know any songs. I can sing you the *Sholoim ale-ichem* and *Tsur misheloy* and perhaps a few others, but that's about it," he said on our way to his home. "I agreed to do the recording only because in this way, we can see each other. In the synagogue we don't have time. Now tell me, what has happened in your lives since we last met? It's too bad you are already leaving! When will you come again?"

Our session ended when he looked at his watch and realized that his guests would be arriving at any moment. The tape captures him saying, in a soft, gentle voice: "Oh, how I lost track of time! We were having such a great time that I forgot about my guests. It's all right, no problem… It's all right if they find you here. You can stay … only … I can't be like this … I have to shave…"

I do not know why these words move me every time I play the tape. His last sentence says more than it seems to say. It is like a song: the memory, the sign and the map.

Estranged

In 1979, after more than a year of seclusion in the forest, I resumed my fieldwork. I slipped back into a routine that seemed like a long lost home—recording sessions and services. The communities embraced me, the lost child, without a word of reproach. I told no one about my plan to leave the country; this information would have been dangerous to both them and for me. Nobody in the community knew that the fall of 1980 would be the last time I joined them for Shabes and *shalashides*, Rosh Hashana and Yom Kippur.

How can I say goodbye? "You Jews, you always…" Yes, we always … we never find our place. We roam in the dusk, chasing dreams in entangled corridors, in the mazes of cold drafts and abandoned stations. In the middle of the journey, we leave and return to where we came from, but home does not feel like home anymore. We fancy that one day we will be like *them*, as if we had forgotten that for a long time, since we first breathed the odor of their meadows and cities and heard the music of their rains and foliage, we have been like them. But no, perhaps not quite…

I wander through magical Budapest. I enter the Dohány Street synagogue; within the hollows of its superabundant stucco ornaments, memories echo like the noise of the sea in a shell thrown ashore. Later, I find myself on a narrow street in front of a secret prayer house. The door has been left open; I enter, the hall is empty. Heaps of tattered prayer books cover the last row of benches, and, suspended in the limitless void, haunts the reverberation of *davenen*. I hear little puffs of snoring—it must be Mr. Waldman, falling asleep during prayers like he did once during the *sliches*, the morning penitential prayer.

My city is as complete as only a city that forever lives on the brink of disintegration can be. The photographs I took on my journey: an empty window frame placed against a wall in front of another wall; a broken crimson velvet armchair leaning against a trashcan; abandoned buckets frozen in the snow. My recordings: a Hassid's hysterical moaning, the dry crackle of a late afternoon *Kaddish*, the barely audible mutter of the

morning prayer. Nothing is what it was *before*. Still, the *whole* is intact and transparent. The fragments speak eloquently, if you only listen.

I have walked for hours and days and years in this city, and I still do not know where my home is. From the perspective of the miserable Jewish courtyards in the seventh district, the palaces of bourgeois Lipótváros appear ridiculous and bombastic, and even the relatively modest apartment buildings in my parents' neighborhood seem like pathetic attempts to look normal. The deeper I sink into one kind of Jewish life, the more absurd the other becomes. I have long made peace with the different lifestyles, arguments and counterarguments, but in the end only the confusion of the heart remains.

Prayer is not born from faith, its music not born from the sound of words. It springs up from depths that are unaccounted for "when, in a furtive moment, the tree roots thirst for speech, when past crumbles upon past and old stories and primeval myths harden, when, under the grass, inarticulate lava thickens and the breath-broken darkness that is prior to all words erupts…" From the realm of the unknowable, a soft and delicate voice calls out: you have no home. You are a stranger in your city and a stranger in your room. A stranger in tradition, in faith, in the sounds. Prayer: being without a home in the world.

"Then the whole crowd burst again into feverish sobs. Candles flickered, scarves fluttered, and in the twilight a group of bald heads emerged, their exhausted martyred foreheads glinting like tarnished silver, their eyes staring stiffly at some remote bliss. The tension exploded in superhuman sound-storms; the sharp staccato of female shrieks lit up the confused darkness of the rasping baritones like lightening over nocturnal steppes. And in the depths of this frenetic delirium, hunger was haunting, hunger was pleading. Then, suddenly, the ram's horn sounded."

(Dezső Szomory, "Yom Kippur," 1925, translation by Ben Niran)

The events of that last autumn brimmed over normal time with endgames of farewells treading on one another. I felt an almost childlike desire to be part of a community that I could acknowledge as mine. I longed for the Seminary's cozy Friday evening services, when I did not have to hide behind the curtain.

I wanted to check something in the library. Since it closed early on Fridays, I was in the building already at noon. I ran up to the second floor in order to take a look at the hall, of which I had such fond memories. Ever since we moved out to the forest, I had stopped attending Friday *Kiddush*, Professor Scheiber's weekly lectures, missing the ritual of the *chala* bread flying over our heads like shooting stars, a testimony to the professor's impressively precise aim.

Preparations for the *Kiddush* had not yet started. The hall, which also held a small library, was completely empty. It showed signs of a recent, thorough cleaning: the floor was shining and spotless and the chairs were on the tables, their legs pointing upward in uniform lines. This meticulous orderliness produced in me an awkward feeling of *déjà vu*; a vague sense of having failed to do something I should have done a long time ago, a failure I could no longer make up for.

I am the first to arrive at the prayer hall. I sit down in my usual seat and watch how the rows of benches fill up with people. The prayer hall is divided into imaginary kingdoms. The older men occupy the first rows and with the murmur of their prayer create

an invisible wall around them. I look for Mr. Waldman, but I do not see him—where could he be? To the left of the *bima* are the benches for the rabbinical students, Emmanuel among them; the chairs on the right are reserved for the professors. Professor Scheiber notices me. He greets me with a nod and elbows his way toward me in the crowd, waving a fat book in his hand. "I just received this, it might interest you. Have a look—but don't forget to give it back after the service..." I put my prayer book aside and begin to flip through Eric Werner's musicological study, *A Voice Still Heard...*

In the first rows, men and women sit separately, but the rules loosen toward the back of the hall. There is always tumult near the entrance, where latecomers block the way. This is the territory of youth: couples stand locked in an embrace, a prayer book in their free hand, although most of them know nothing of the religion and do not read Hebrew. For the most part, they do not let their conversation be disturbed by the service, but every now and then—for instance when the rabbinical students begin to sing—they relax their embrace, open the prayer book (usually on the wrong page) and make an attempt to join in with the choir. In Jewish circles, as well as at the police headquarters, it is no secret that the seminary's Friday night ritual and the following *Kiddush* function as a dating service.

The balcony is reserved for the specialists: members of the choir and their ever-growing circle of friends and relatives. The parterre abounds in the happy cacophony of mispronounced Hebrew words, but on the balcony, order reigns. Like the captain of a ship caught in a storm, the organist bravely attempts to impose some structure on the chaos, and with a jovial grin sprinkles sweet harmonies on every melody he can lay his hands on. The cantor, in normal circumstances a good musician, proclaims truth with whining melodies bellowed across the hall in a rich bass voice that could fill a stadium.

The people in the first rows stand up. The insiders whisper to the newcomers that the *Shemone esre* is about to begin. The young couples are clueless as to what is going on, but they sense that it must be something serious and briefly stop talking. There is silence in the room, and only the gentle murmurs of the elderly are heard—those who know that the *Shemone esre* should be recited with great concentration and in a whispering and barely audible voice. I stand up, close Eric Werner's book, open my *siddur* and begin to pray. The hall is filled with the wondrous solemnity of the rustling of *davenen*.

Suddenly, sweet chords pour down from the organ. Every Friday, the organist plays the same piece to accompany the silent prayer of *Shemone esre*. This bittersweet composition, with its harmonic clichés and romantic suspensions—an atmosphere so different from the subdued and mysterious whispering of *davenen*—has always annoyed me. The moment the song begins, the waves of *davenen* are trapped and the miracle evaporates.

But now, perhaps because I know that I am hearing it for the last time, my resistance melts. In the waves of perspiration of the excited bodies, under the warm yellow light of the chandeliers and the shimmering colors of the glass window, here and now and among them, this trivial composition becomes grand. Standing together below the sound of the organ, we finally seem to notice ourselves and wake up to the realization that this is really happening; that we, the dwindling remnant of the great Jewish community of Budapest, are *alive*. We, the quarreling and squabbling Jews of Pest, have come together in this room where decades ago our fathers stood, searching for the reverberation of fears in the eyes, shelter in these melodies. And when, above the sound of the organ, the students begin to sing the *Elaihenu*, a warm shiver goes through my body and in the depths of my heart a childish and never completely silenced voice cries out: I want to be *one among them*.

But later, at home, the memory of this evening has a stale aftertaste. I almost feel as if I just attended an orgy. What does it matter? I calm myself—I am not religious. But matchmaking under the pretext of prayer… No… that is too much. One has to draw the line somewhere. If this sentimental hocus-pocus is necessary in order to belong, then I would rather not belong. I won't give in to the atavistic beliefs of secret tribes, the secret call of our forefathers, or blood brotherhoods.

Yet is it not the rule of the game in life that sooner or later we "give in" to something? I tread the miles carved out for me by my ancestors—the road between Orthodoxy and assimilation, Communism and religion, blood brotherhood and loneliness. Again and again, I knock down my pawns in the checkmate game of Jewish life.

The following Shabes, I decide to go to the Kazinczy Street synagogue. This synagogue wants no newcomers and no converts; it promises no quick redemption. They throw the truth right into your face: you are not welcome. They know you don't really mean it: you won't open your heart and go all the way into the dark, mad ecstasy of faith. Not even your grandfather did, so what business do you have being here?

I make a point of arriving early, so I can spend some time on my own. I enter the men's section on the ground floor, naturally without permission. I hide in a dark corner near the wall, holding my breath so as not to disturb the spirits I always felt have haunted this structure. Reality recedes, and the dream of another life spreads its wings above my head.

Since I am the first person here, I have to ask for the gate to the stairway to be opened. The stairs lead to the women's galleries on the second and third floors. My request is met with a doubtful look, since women do not come so early for the service. Wooden balustrades, blocking the view of the ground floor, enclose the galleries. If you lay your head on two columns of the balustrade, eyes so close that, on the sides of your vision, the shapes of the columns become blurred, you can peak though the opening. In this slim vertical niche appear, like a mirage in the distance, the illuminated ground floor, carved wooden benches, flowery wall paint and a chandelier—a miniature painting of an oriental temple in a fairytale. The precision of this splinter view of a wondrous space framed by darkness of the columns on both sides—this is the image that

my memory retained and that has become, for me, the paradigm of prayer: a thin strip of clarity torn from darkness.

I choose a bench and began to read the prayers. The sound of my own whisper comes back to me like an alien voice, and slowly, I doze off. In my dream, I stand at the entrance of a house. I climb a spiral staircase. Although it does not resemble this building, I am certain that the stairs lead to Roth's apartment. I begin to look for his door, up and down, almost running. Suddenly, I come to a landing in an open corridor, across which a massive, windowless brick wall looms like a prohibition. Light pours over me and I plunge, as if from great heights, into the pale white sky. I am falling or perhaps ascending at tremendous speed until, at the verge of waking, my ascent becomes an effortless gliding over distant lands. In a state of semi-consciousness, I force my mind to retain the sensation of weightless flight, and I realize that all along I had been hearing a delicate singing voice, which had stopped forever as I rose from the familiar stairwell above alien clouds.

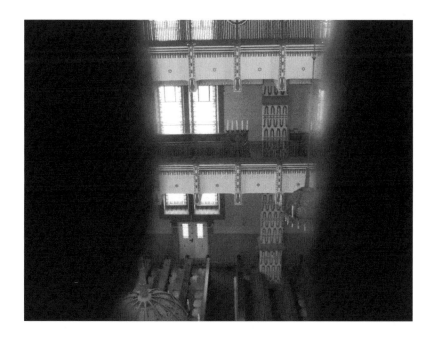

When I awake, I find myself between a mumbling old lady and a younger, seemingly deranged woman who is swaying her body vehemently; they must have arrived while I was asleep. On the ground floor, the men are already reciting their prayers. From the chaos of their recitations, sparks of scorched whisper, sobbing and moaning rise up to the gallery, and from the far corner flows a delicate, almost lifeless voice, like that of a lost child. Later, at home, I write in my diary: "I was at Kazinczy today. Whisper. Voices. Ash. Loneliness."

The *davenen* recedes, the people stand up, turn eastward and begin to pray the *Shemone esre*. Although I see only waving backs, I sense the passion that is streaming from their eyes. Devotion pulsates in the air, throbs in my temples, I should be praying. But I am just standing there, prayer book in my hand, paralyzed by the stifled fervor of their concentration.

I recall the warm sensation I had during the *Shemone esre* at the Rabbinical Seminary, with its lulling organ music, and I lower my head in shame. I hastily begin to read the prayer. The men have already finished; the intensity loosens, and fragments of conversation float up to the gallery. Then, at last, the cantor's singing relieves the anguish of our loneliness.

I sit down. I am exhausted, as if I had been running for hours. It feels good to listen to the cantor without thinking about anything. The women have already resumed their chatter. I cannot recall the organ music, but the memory of its atmosphere still haunts me. The seminary's nervous efforts to create a community through union in prayer now appear laughable. In Kazinczy Street, standing between a lethargic and a crazy woman, I realize that what I had felt there was betrayal. Here, they know that the sense of belonging is an illusion. Nobody stands with you in prayer. You are alone. Before God and before yourself: you are alone.

I stand again at the bolted gateway. I cross the courtyard, climb up the damp stairwell and open the door to the secret, little *shul* for the last time.

I arrive in the afternoon, before anyone else. I choose a place near the *bima* from where I can take in the entire hall, along with a full view of my curtain from the other side—the men's section. In the dim light, the plaster-white *kitl* thrown casually on a chair in front of the curtain looks like a bizarre antique sculpture. The light from the window, the framed calligraphic inscriptions on the back wall, the simple chandelier and the white stripes of the prayer books on the dark wooden desks—everything seems heartrendingly familiar. It is as though I happened upon the point of stillness in the ceaseless bustle of life. This little room is the ultimate station of serenity—there is nothing beyond it. I suddenly realize my terrible loss. After I leave, nothing will ever be the same.

It seems as if today the voices of *davenen* abound with particular intensity. Still, the atmosphere is different from the dark passions of Kazinczy Street. In this little *shul*, prayer unfolds gently and spontaneously. It is like the lilting of morning birds, an agglomeration of desires without master, little bruised spirits catapulting their throbbing song into the swarm.

In a traditional *shul*, you do not join in—you tear out a piece of territory for yourself. You fence off a corridor of silence into which you pour out the story that swells up from the padlocked cage within. You are left on your own to do whatever you want: pray, dream or sink.

But your loneliness is not complete. Codes of indecipherable hieroglyphs are all around you, and the roles seem to be enacted according to a secret libretto. I could never figure out what *I* was allowed, or supposed, to do. Everybody prayed differently—one man screamed, another barely moved his lips, one with melody, the other speaking. Everyone behaved differently: one constantly talked, the other was late, and another made noise with his chair. But this did not mean that you were allowed to do whatever you wished. There was an old man who, a few minutes into the prayer, began to scream and weep. But when it occurred to another man to do the same, he was told, politely but firmly, to "stop right now." I, too, felt the screaming of the first man to be real, and

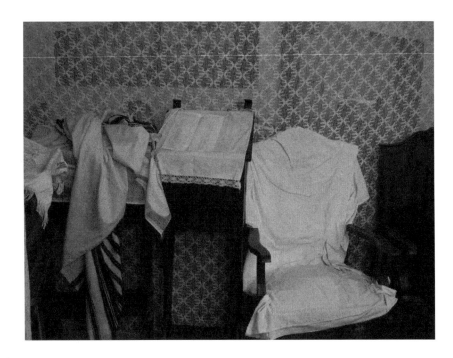

that of the second—a show. You are granted a space, any space, in principle, but you have to fill it with *your* voice. Nobody will tell you how to do that.

The service is a sonorous apparition in *your* ears: the sound of whatever you are living through, the ritual you create for yourself. You listen to voices, coming from within and without, and you alone can decide which one from among the sound-souls will enter the empire of your prayer. It is a ritual even if you don't pray. Then, it is the sound ritual of not-praying-only-listening or of the letting-it-happen-in-the-background-to-daydreaming. Do as you wish; the sound takes you even without your will; it pulls and pushes until from the ravines of the soul your inner voice awakens—the voice that you denied and dared not trust.

Suddenly, it dawns on me that I am less of an outsider than I had thought. For a long time now, I have not made any particular effort to remain invisible. I allow the paper to rustle when I unpack a prayer book and cross the men's section to get to the shelf if I need another one. The men neither stop me nor encourage me. Some seem to look through me, but others smile, speak to me and pray for me—it is all very natural. During the service, I breathe my high-pitched little melodies, hesitant and bizarre smoke rings, into their cloud. I let my voice muddle their well-rehearsed theater. I have never been told to stop. Their service has become what it is because I am among them. They will miss me.

I find myself at the banks of the Danube. I leaf through the book of memories and a photo emerges: my parents, brother and I cuddling at the Margaret Bridge after the Sunday ice-cream walk. Suppressed dreams erupt and apparitions of past things flutter on the canvas of the sky, they draw and entice, and I turn onto the bridge toward Margaret Island. What am I doing? I have thousands of urgent errands to settle before the trip. You cannot bid farewell to every corner and every stone.

I reach the ruins of the cloister and wander around the stones. Life was so simple when grandmother took my brother and me to play here. No theories were needed, no proofs. Fantasy unfolded effortlessly: this heap of stones is the wall of the waiting room, here is the dining hall, and over there are the cells of the nuns. See: here sleeps Saint Margaret. In the blossoming fantasy of the child, the stones multiply, transform and get entangled, and myriads of potential floor plans take shape under our feet. It is simple, easy and self-evident.

Hurry up, it's almost dark—grandmother is ready to go. All right, allow us one last jump from the top of the wall to the kitchen, because it is always warm there. They used to cook big quantities of food for the needy, or so we read in the explanation, while the rest of the cloister remained cold, and in the winter the nuns were literally freezing.

I begin to hum the beautiful antiphon *Dum fabricator mundi.* I remember the text only vaguely, and sing abracadabra for those parts that have faded from my memory. I would prefer to whistle the tune, if only I could whistle. How many more things are there for me to learn: whistle, skate, ride a bicycle, dance the tango, Hebrew, Aramaic, and other amazing languages! Paris will be the first station on my journey. I will deepen my knowledge of Gregorian chant at the Sorbonne and perhaps even research the manuscripts in the library of the famous Abbey of Solesmes. How much I love this—and this, and this too!

It cannot be otherwise. We are given two legs in order to stand at six hundred and thirteen different places at the same time. A person's life is here and there and also over there. I will set out on my great expedition with two suitcases jammed with books, tapes, anxieties and expectations, puppet theaters and labyrinths. Yes, *Dum fabricator mundi,* that is how it is, *mortis supplicium,* be patient, *pateretur in cruce,* I will get to you, too, *clamans voce magna.* There are only a few weeks left till the journey. But before I leave, I want to make a last attempt to understand what apparently nobody has tried to understand: the mad system of *davenen.*

Kazinczy Street has never accepted me. Still, I go there for Yom Kippur before I leave my country. I arrive when it is still dark and climb up to the third floor to be on my own for a while. Then, carefully, so that nobody can see where I come from, I descend to the second floor gallery. The women there scrutinize me, perhaps my face is not sufficiently pallid. Too polite to ask whether or not I am keeping the fast, the most religious among the women stay away from me altogether. Needless to say, I have not eaten or drunk since the previous day, but it is none of their business and I don't care what they think. Let's pretend I am a traveller who chanced upon this superstitious, backward village by accident. I touch the pencil in my pocket. It is forbidden to write on holidays.

The building is in a dismal state. On the gallery, where we pray, the floor is strewn with parts of broken benches. Before you sit down, it is necessary to check whether the seat is not going to disintegrate at first touch. I choose a place next to a round and sympathetic looking woman.

At my seat, the desk for the prayer book is almost intact. There is a small golden nameplate nailed to it: "Aranka Goldberger." I am sitting in Aranka Goldberger's seat. I glance at my neighbor. From her gestures, I can tell she has lived her entire life in the Kazinczy Street *shtetl*. I cautiously ask her whether she knew Aranka. "What do you want?" she barks at me. I nod at the nameplate: "Aranka Goldberger. Did you know her?" She signals with a frown that she doesn't want to be bothered. A few minutes later, she puts her hand on my arm: "See the fat man with the golden *kipa* standing near the door? He's the only one from the Goldberger family who came back." Not waiting for my response, she turns around and lapses into murmuring.

I gaze at the painted flowers that adorn the ceiling and the walls in continuous, densely placed squares. What are such happy, innocent designs doing in a house of terrifying rituals?

It is hard to imagine that this synagogue was once filled with people, shimmering in the brilliant light of chandeliers. Two galleries with hundreds of seats were needed to accommodate the women alone, meaning that, at the beginning of the twentieth century, an Orthodox community the size of a village lived its secluded life in the heart of downtown Budapest.

This is my Kazinczy Street: a small, dwindling and embittered community, decayed walls covered with a thick residue of smoke and dust, pieces of plaster falling from the ceiling. And all around: sadness. But if I stay here long enough, reality, like a thin membrane, breaks open. Images of gently waving prayer shawls, gold and blue embroidery on the *kipas*, colored flowers on the wall behind layers of dust—in these desolate fragments the past vibrates, images emerge, decompose, molder and assemble anew, they glitter and sparkle in the deep flight of fantasy. I see and hear the Yom Kippur of the past: the hall is packed, the air vibrates, the painted flowers gleam, and in the candle-light, from under the blue-white waves of the prayer shawls, the mysterious steam of prayer rises up toward the skies.

Matter decays; only the moment's flight in your pupil is eternal. At dawn, during the first whisper of prayer, a red light beam flares up, and for a moment floods the hall. Once, before the apocalypse, at exactly this moment in the service, in exactly this place—my place—stood a girl. Mesmerized by the beauty of the sudden red light and shuddering at the fervor of the prayer, she looked at the wall and wondered: "What are such happy, innocent designs doing in a house of terrifying rituals?" And she felt what I feel now: we are protected. The sound of prayer thickens around us; it covers and hides and takes us away on its wings. It does not matter whether we pray or think of something else or think of nothing. The murmur prays for us.

I close my *machzor* and go towards the door. The floorboards creak under my feet; you cannot leave unnoticed. The door slams and the women shake their heads in dis-approval. I lean onto the cool wall of the corridor and wait until I calm down. I begin to climb the stairs to the third floor. According to the women, the third floor gallery is in an even worse state than the rest of the building. "Don't ever go up there! It's danger-ous." I enter the gallery and close the door behind me as silently as possible.

Clearly, nobody has used this gallery for decades. Chunks of plaster are scattered on the floor, and with every step new pieces fall down from the ceiling. Earlier, I sat in the first row, but now I choose a place in the back, far from the balustrade, so that I won't be seen from below. There is a small golden nameplate on the desk, reminding me that here, too, I am taking someone else's place. I remove the larger pieces of debris from the seat and place the prayer book on the white layer of pulverized plaster, which, like thin autumn snow, covers everything. My hair and clothes are grey from the dust floating all around. I wipe it from the golden plate, feeling the particles between my fingers.

I take the pencil and notebook from my pocket and begin to murmur along with the sounds from below. I try to detect the basic melody underlying the individual chanting voices, each of which brings its unique variant. When it seems like I found it, I write it down, then listen again and notate, page upon page.

I leave the hall in order to check my notations. Adjacent to the bathrooms, there is a dilapidated room whose original purpose is impossible to determine. Inside it, the silence is complete. It is not difficult to reproduce the notes on the paper, but when

I sing them from my transcription the melodies sound flat, empty and boring. By now, I know why: as long as I sing precise pitches and comprehensible rhythms, I won't sound like them. This is not how *they* sing. Their melodies are muddy and chaotic, chilling splinters of cries, bleating and moaning, a jumble of wretched and howling outbursts and proclamations. Inside the prayer hall, there is no music, only spirit … *ruach* and *ruach* … wind and rain and river, the rustle of the foliage in deep forests, the roar of waterfalls, the sizzle of burning wood...

I return to the hall. I concentrate. I try to memorize the subtleties of the rhythms, the ornaments and the shades of these voices. But slowly, I am taken over by fatigue. What is the point? Why should I care? Let them pray as they please, even if I will never understand. I will pray *my way*; I might as well pray since I am here. I put the pencil and notebook into my pocket and begin to mutter the words as they are printed in the book. An hour passes, then another, then more and more immeasurable hours until I am dizzy with ecstasy, fatigue and hunger. I howl and bleat and whine; the sounds erupt from my mouth uncontrollably—crooked and sick and hunchbacked and miserable melodies, twitching and writhing and falling.

I gather my strength and go back to my secret room. But it is as though my Jewish voice departs the moment I leave them. As if an invisible wall, which the sound of faith cannot breach, encloses the prayer hall.

I cannot take it any longer. I need fresh air. I leave the synagogue and wander aimlessly outside. It is afternoon. Suddenly I find myself in front of the Academy of Music. I am skipping class today under the pretext of being sick. I look up at the magnificent façade, trying to guess what might be going on behind the windows. I am perplexed that the building is standing at all and that inside it people are eating and practicing. As though I were seeing it for the first time, the building seems alien, cruel and sly, something to be on guard against. Fainting from hunger, I drag myself down Mayakovsky Street to the Boulevard. A cascade of colors greets me; amid the deafening roar of construction, people, cars and trams seem to glide by with terrifying speed, and in a shop window I catch the reflection of a violently laughing couple. It is a nightmare. I stand deaf and dumb at the corner of Dohány Street as if I arrived today from some small prayer room in a village in the middle of nowhere.

It is already evening when I return to the synagogue. I find my place and sit down next to the round woman. The shadows are deeper now; the light from the chandeliers flickers like fire. The sound, too, is transformed. In the afternoon the murmur was pale and grey, broken voices colliding like waves on a disturbed lake. At the end of the day it is like a dark, trembling whisper, a shimmer of deep blue and reddened gold from the bottom of the ocean. Even with my eyes closed, I would know that night is approaching. These are the sounds of the last exertion, the soul's final leap into madness, into repentance that shames and that one is ashamed of.

Rabbi Weiss sings the *nile*. It is said of him that before he begins the final *Ovini malkeini*, he takes out his watch. He recites the last line at the exact moment the holiday ends, so that the people do not need to fast more than is necessary. Self-control and proportion in ecstasy. His *Ovini malkeini* burns, the lines sway in pain and sorrow, they flare up toward the heights of ineffable sadness, then with a last flicker they die away. Even if all were lost, without anything left to believe in, this truth remains: Moshe Weiss's *nile* voice hovering in the ether.

The crowd responds with a feverish sob that shakes the hall like the battle cry of a wild tribe. Tension explodes in superhuman sound-storms; sharp female shrieks, like lightning over nocturnal steppes, illuminate the confused darkness of the men's rasping prayer. In the depths of this frenetic delirium, hunger is haunting and pleading. Then, finally, the shofar sounds.

It is over. Rabbi Weiss sings the closing *Kaddish* to an insignificant little tune. This banal song is the frontier between heaven and earth, between mystery and the everyday. It is the seal on the book of golden memory of things past. Repentance and ecstasy, too, have an end: you must know how to go beyond, and how to come back. Until this point, go no further.

I wait for most of the congregation to leave in order to sneak into the men's section and look at the hall one last time. I prepare myself for the journey from Kazinczy Street to Újlipótváros, where my parents are expecting me for dinner. Back in Újlipótváros, I will once again be one among *them* (the other *them*)—for whom Yom Kippur and fasting are the remnants of an unfortunate superstition. I will return to life—to the Academy of Music. Along with others like me, I will continue to ride the waves back and forth: enlightened one day, withdrawn into a shell the next, each moment longing to be wherever we are not.

In the meantime, the atmosphere in the synagogue has changed. In the front of the hall, a few men recite the regular evening prayer tiredly and mechanically. Others talk, joke and discuss business; nobody entering now would believe that these same people had been weeping and screaming only a minute earlier. I step into the courtyard, where people are chatting. One man beckons to me. He showers me with good wishes, offers me a plastic cup filled with a dubious, strong smelling liquid, and piles a heap of sweet pastries into my open palm.

II. Voices

"If You Are Moved by the Living ..."

"Marci" (Márton Fóti, Mordechai ben Shlomo Jechiel, 1992–1999)

"It is difficult to describe what Shabes meant to us to someone who did not live through it. I often ask myself what made it so special. There was something in the air, a feeling... I never feel this today."

"My mother would begin cooking on Thursday. She was a wonderful cook; it was real art what she made for us. The preparations began on Thursday—actually on

Wednesday, counting the shopping—and this whole period was filled with an air of expectancy. From Thursday on … in fact, the entire week … we were preparing ourselves practically and spiritually for Shabes. We spent any free time we had studying the portion of the Torah assigned for that week. During the entire week, Shabes was always in the back of our minds. We imagined the candlesticks, the light, the clean room, the beautiful table, and the nice clothes we were going to wear."

"We helped my mother; each of us had a special task. It was important that we did not leave her alone. Even so, she worked terribly, terribly hard. I remember for instance that my father had the task of preparing a kind of goose liver pâté. My mother cooked the liver, but the rest was my father's task and this had to be done at the last moment, on Friday afternoon. That pâté, which was delicious, by the way, needed freshly chopped onions. My father cut onions so fast and fine that none of us could understand how he did it. This onion cutting was his specialty, which he performed ritually every Friday afternoon."

"When on Friday night we came home from *shul* and sat around the table … that was a special moment. We were relaxed and paid attention to everything—the food, the conversation and the songs. We did not have to hurry or think of errands … that I forgot to do this or that and how much work was waiting for me tomorrow. We had the whole evening, the whole night and the whole next day to ourselves. And it seemed as if during the entire week we had been living only for this evening."

"My father sang the *zmires*. He knew all their verses by heart. We joined in for some of the songs, but at other times we just listened. He had a special style. He sang as if he were telling a story. He withdrew into himself, afraid, almost, of being at the center of attention. It was so modest, so … how should I say it … unpretentious, that you had to listen."

"Someone who has not lived through these things cannot understand… It is impossible to explain that feeling of … warmth … there is no better word … blessedness … a feeling of blessedness. And even if many of us did not keep the religion, at least not in that rigid form, the experience remained for life. It is alive in me to this day."

"On Shabes morning I would play soccer in an empty lot adjacent to the synagogue. That was what interested me most in those days—kicking the ball. I loved soccer. My older brothers had to be at the service from the beginning, but the little ones were allowed to play. This was all right with my father as long as we were inside for the silent *tfile*, the *Shemone esre*. If by then we were not lined up nicely at his side, with our *siddurs* in hand and open on the right page … well … that was bad—it meant spanking. So, every so often one of us would go in to check their progress. Of course, it was always at more or less the same time, but a wristwatch was a rare thing in those days, and certainly not something for children, so we needed a scout to report which part of the prayer was read inside at any given time. We were supposed to enter the hall during the prayer that preceded this silent prayer, the silent *tfile* and line up at my father's side without making noise; we sneaked in on tippy toes and without a word, and this was not easy. Sometimes my father was so immersed in prayer that he did not notice when we came in. He looked around only before the *Shemone esre* to check that we were there, and we were all right. Before he began his prayer, he put his hand on our heads and caressed us one by one. That was how the service began for me on Shabes: feeling my father's hand on my head."

"Ours was a lively town with many Jews, quite a few of whom were rather well off. There were two synagogues and several prayer houses. Our family belonged to the modern community. My father was strictly religious and he would have fit in better with the Orthodox congregation, but he preferred the moderns and most of his friends came from that circle. The Orthodox *kihle* was too rigid for him, and he felt uncomfortable with the way they prayed, because they were 'chasing the words,' or so he used to say. But the modern *kihle* was problematic for other reasons, and actually, we did not pray with them either. In that essentially modern congregation there were others like him, people who, although they preferred to belong to the moderns, wanted to pray more seriously, for instance without omitting any of the texts. They formed an inner circle within the congregation. They continued to pray in the same building but, instead of the big hall, in the smaller study room."

"They could have simply left the congregation and formed a community of their own. But they did not want to, because they liked this congregation; they only wanted to pray a bit differently, with a different tempo and atmosphere. And nobody thought this was a problem. There was no hostility between this inner group and the rest—at least, this was my feeling as a child. And this was the most wonderful thing, because there were two worlds around me. When we prayed in the small room, we could hear the noise coming from the main hall. During the silent *tfile*, we could hear that they were already at another section in the prayer, and I suppose they also heard us during their silent *tfile*. This was my childhood: the melodies of our prayer room and around it the noise of the larger community. I felt doubly protected."

"I arrived in Pest in the 1930s, and it is where I came back to after the war. I settled at the little prayer house on Vörösmarty Street. It was a special community. All of us had had a good religious education and knew what all this was about and how things were done before the war. I wanted to show you a photograph that was taken at *Simches taire* some time in the eighties, a few years before the community dissolved; I saw it lying around just the other day, but I cannot find it. It is a truly historic photograph. As far as I remember, I am on the left holding the Torah, and Steinberg, the *rashekol*, and Hari are also in the picture. Ask Hari to show it to you, he also has a copy."

"During the Communist period, I went to *shul* secretly. I was the director of a branch of the machine manufacturing industry—actually, a separate little factory I had established after the war, entirely on my own, and which the Communists took away, nationalized and merged into a large cooperative. After some initial turbulence, I became the director of the branch that was originally my factory. I did not own it any longer, but still, this was a good deal because at least I was free to skip work and go to *shul* on the Jewish holidays. Early in the morning I would rush to the factory, say I had an urgent errand to run in the central office and did not know when I would be back. Of course, I did not go back because I was praying all day. I worked overtime on other days and also

on Sundays; it was a well-functioning and successful factory and we worked around the clock. But no matter how much one worked, it was impossible to say … not even the director could have said, 'I'm sorry, today is a fast day and I must go and *daven*.'"

"It wasn't easy to be Jewish in those days. But on the whole, those decades after the war and also today … even though the religion, at least in its old form, is gone … our lives are better today. For all its beauty, religion as I remember it had its dark sides. It was oppressive, especially for the women. And for the children—yes, especially for the children! We had to get up at five in the morning, go to *cheider* and then run to get to school by eight. In the afternoon: *cheider* again. Of course we walked to school also in winter, the snow up to our knees. We collapsed into bed late at night, and apart from that little soccer on Shabes morning, we didn't have a moment to breathe, let alone play. It was torture."

"In those days, learning meant memorizing; you had to repeat the texts until they stuck in your head. We could sing the prayers perfectly already as small children, without having the faintest notion of what the words meant. There were no translations and no explanations. Don't ask questions, just pray! The words were abracadabra, they meant whatever you imagined, their sound and melody—fortunately, there were melodies. If you were clever and motivated, you figured out the meaning, first a word here and there, then fragments and sentences. Of course, we discussed it among ourselves, and actually, by the time we finished school we understood most of it … more or less. At *cheider*, although we were only four or five years old when we went there, the focus was on the Torah, which we translated and explained. The teacher took it for granted that the rest was already behind us; you were already supposed to know the prayers."

"The idea was that you should *feel* the meaning of the text from the sound of the words. A child is not sufficiently mature to descend into the depths of these texts and process them intellectually and emotionally. When you are ready, you will understand. Because the meaning … the *real meaning* … the essence of a prayer … cannot be translated or explained—it is something inexpressible. One day, it dawns on you … it hits you. You understand by yourself … only by yourself can you understand."

"Well, there is some truth in this idea. But the method that leads you there is torturous. Today, it is impossible to push children through such a system … thank God!"

"In those days, when I was the director of the company, I began to collect cantorial recordings. You could find them all over the place, thrown out with other rubbish in abandoned lots, in waste bins, and sometimes even in record stores. I had almost no experience with cantorial music. I had heard cantors in Budapest, but I spent only a year here before the war broke out. Of course, I knew the *nusach*, but these melodies were different; they were somehow … fantastic."

"At home, in secret, I listened to these records and sang along with them. I began to compose pieces by mixing what I knew from home with the ideas I heard on these records. It became my secret hobby, composing cantorial pieces and singing them to myself at home. I developed a whole repertory—full services, which I did not dare show to anybody. Then one day—this was already here, at the Hunyadi Square synagogue—I was asked to lead the service. People knew that I brought the traditional *nusach* from home, from before the war. I took a deep breath and decided to sing these fantasies instead of the simple *nusach*. I was prepared for a phenomenal scandal. Instead, it turned out to be a great success. This is how I became a cantor at the age of sixty-four."

"Here, at the Hunyadi Square synagogue, we used to divide the tasks on Shabes, like it is done in most communities. Hari did the musically simpler section, the *psuke dezimra*, and I sang the cantorial parts of the *shachris* and the *musaf*. Since Hari left for the synagogue on Károlyi Gáspár Square, we are in big trouble. He knew so much; it is impossible to replace him."

"You want to know how I compose? Early in the morning in the prayer house. Our *shul* is on the second floor, and its windows face the market square. I like to buy things there. On Shabes, when I cross the market, I often think that it would be nice to do some shopping, since I am here anyway. But of course, this is forbidden on Shabes.

I come early, before anybody else, and begin to read the texts. I read and read, and then, suddenly, I look out the window, and over the lace curtains, I notice the square. In winter, I watch the people drag themselves through snow to reach the market. And even though it is my market, it seems distant. I even feel sorry for them, those people outside: how awful it must be to have to calculate prices, decide and bargain, and how wonderful it is that I can be alone with these texts. It's then that the ideas come."

"Take this prayer, for instance. One reads it every morning; it's nothing special. But one day, you suddenly understand. It suddenly means something to you; it strikes you like lightning, moves you in a way you never imagined. If you are a prayer leader, you have to make something of this understanding—you have to say it in music. But, then, the people should listen. I don't care for these modest prayer leaders who never think about themselves. One has to be a bit selfish. When I pray, there is no talking in the prayer house. They listen only to me."

"Éva" (Mrs. Éva Oberländer, née Rosenberg, 1993–1994)

"Yes … here … in this very spot … I stood here the whole day, the same way I stood a minute ago when we recorded the Shabes *tfile*. I wish I could go to the synagogue, but my legs won't carry me any more. I have to hold the service for myself at home."

"On the day of *Yomkiper* I would get up at six in the morning, go outside to feed the chickens, then wash and make space, here, on the table, and begin the prayers for the fast day. But this year I promised myself that I would drink and eat and take my medication the moment I felt sick. I have no telephone. If I faint or die, nobody will notice, so I have to be careful. Before seven, I was already standing here with the prayer book in my hand. I began reading the prayers the way you should, with their melodies. I *davened* one prayer after the other, and suddenly I saw the pages become grey and the letters disappear—it had become dark and I was already in the *nile* at the *Ovini malkei-ni*. I did not even notice the day go by. The Almighty was with me: I stood here, at the table, the whole day, and not for a moment did I feel weak or hungry. Here alone, at this spot…"

"Once you get used to these things, it's not difficult. In fact, for me, it would have been harder to eat on *Yomkiper*. To break the rules, which I had never, ever done in my life… It would have felt as though, at that moment, breaking the rules, my old life had ended."

"We had a good life, a very good life in my village. I'm not saying this because I am nostalgic, but because I really think it was a better life. We knew what was important and were able to judge the value of things. Look, here it is, for instance, this new rabbi who was sent to us from Budapest; he is very nice, a really lovely boy. The other day, he came to visit me and asked where the toilet was. As you know, I have no toilet. 'Go to the garden, find a place and do what you have to do,' I told him. He stared at me with big eyes, thinking I must be the most miserable person on earth. As if it is a great trag-edy that there is no toilet! I cannot fathom how one could feel heartbroken because of a toilet. Heartbroken and miserable... It's because of people ... because of the people I have lost and because of the life I once had..."

"My father sent all his children to school, the girls too, me and my sisters. When it came to education, he made no distinction between his sons and daughters. He said that the Almighty had planted a soul in every human being and, in his house, there would be no difference. We had to learn everything the boys did. We studied Torah, learned how to sing it with its special melody, which is called *leinen*, and studied the commentaries and explanations. When I tell this to people today, they say that I am senile and making it all up. Nonsense: me, senile! I remember everything as if it were yesterday. But it's true that there weren't many families like ours. In our village, besides us, only the Klein girls studied. The other girls knew the prayers, the holidays, *kashrus* and some songs—that was all. But my father loved us, his daughters, and for him, love meant education. Imagine all this in a little, faraway village! When I think of this, when I think of him and how he died... Oh, my God, how can such a thing ... how such things could be possible..."

"Ours was the most beautiful village I have ever seen. It was a well-to-do village; the land was good and everyone had fields and orchards and animals. It was a hard life, of course; we had to work from dawn till sunset—all the time. And there were no luxuries like toilets or bathrooms or the like. But a river ran behind the houses, and it was clean. Everybody had a garden and people planted flowers by the side of the road and every family took care of the rows of flowers in front of their house. You see, even today, when I can barely walk, I plant flowers... I start each spring with planting flowers. I could use that ground for vegetables, which would be perhaps more practical. But I cannot live without flowers."

"Our village was special. You could count on the people; they helped each other and it made no difference whether you were Christian or Jewish. We played together and learned songs from each other; I used to know dozens of Hungarian songs like the one I sang for you the other day."

"Even the chief of police was a human being, which was not typical in those days. During the war, the Arrow Cross men came to the village and ordered him to round up the Jews. Now, this was not so simple because the village extended through many

miles, as some of the fields lay between the houses and one needed a horse to do the job. Our police chief took his horse from the stable, walked it to the edge of the forest and let it run into the woods. Then he went back and reported to the Arrow Cross men that his horse had run away, so he could not round up the Jews. Then the Arrow Cross men brought help from somewhere else … and they took us all … all … my sisters and friends … my father … my father…"

"Dead, my God, they are all dead! My father, my mother, my aunts, cousins, my sisters and brothers … nobody came back. I am the only one from our village, no other … not a single soul remained from among the Jews. I don't want this, I cannot …

I cannot speak about this, why are you asking these questions about what was then … then … before … stop the tape … I don't want people to hear me crying…"

"I know you mean well, my sweet, my dear Juditka, but there's no point. Nobody has come back from among the people of my village. How will those scholars in the city, when they listen to this, how will they know I am telling the truth? Perhaps I really don't remember any more. Perhaps all this was a dream; perhaps our village and our lives have never been."

A woman in the Hunyadi Square synagogue (1990s)

"On Shabes, I am usually late. When I arrive, the men are already praying. From my home to this *shul*—at my age, that's a distance. When I get up in the morning my whole body aches. I barely go out; I have no need to see people any more. What for? I can say my prayers at home. And to come to this place … well, it's not such a pleasure! The building is completely run down, a dismal sight. Do I want to see this on Shabes? As I climb the stairs, I often think that it would have been better to stay home. But when I reach the door and hear the men praying … as if…"

"I don't enter the prayer room immediately. I sit here in the antechamber, sometimes for a long time. I listen to the sounds and … it seems I have arrived home. The sound of *davenen* … it is like the voices in the prayer house of our village some seventy years ago, when I was a little girl. I know it can't be—I am dreaming. Nobody was left from my village; they killed them all. And still, when I sit here and listen, it sounds as if nothing has happened, as if today is like it has always been, as if it would go on forever."

"Feigele" (Mrs. Magda Szepesi, Feigele Bas Yitzhak Halevi, 2003)

"One day, after my husband and I had retired, we sat down and looked at each other. We both knew what the other was thinking: that from now on, we would keep Shabes. During the Communist times it was impossible not to work on Saturday, but now that we had retired we could do it. But there was no synagogue nearby. We had some savings and bought an apartment, actually, a small house across the park, on the other side of Károlyi Gáspár Square, and with the help of the community and some private donors we converted it into a synagogue. At first, we were afraid it would not work, because it was far from the city center where most Jews lived. But we never had any problems; within a few weeks, many people joined and my husband and I became something like the presidents of the congregation."

"It was a lot of work: the building, the bills, the people, and of course, my husband had to lead the service. Luckily, we managed to convince Hari to be our *baltfile*—it was like winning the lottery! He left the Hunyadi Square synagogue, which was a central place. But I don't think they loved him as much as we do here. At the Hunyadi, they divided the prayers. Marci became a kind of chief cantor; he sang the highlights—those texts that people think need a big voice. The rest was left for Hari to *daven*. With us, it's different. Hari and my husband were a team and there was no competition between them; each was happy to let the other have the spotlight. If one of them was tired, the other sang more; they decided it just before the service, spontaneously, and everything between them was simple and natural. Together they created a wonderful atmosphere. A few years ago my husband died, and now Hari sings the entire service alone, which is too much for him at his age."

"No, Feigele is not my real name—it's Magda, or, as they often call me, Magdi, or Magdika. One day, Hari began calling me Feigele. I did not particularly like the idea and told him to stop. But he just was not capable of calling me Magdi. He said that for my 'heroic deeds' for this community, I deserved to have a real Yiddish name. Now everyone calls me Feigele. Imagine—at the age of seventy-two I got a new name!"

"The most beautiful thing I remember from childhood is *Tishebov*. For the Jews, *Tishebov* is the most important day of mourning—a fast day that occurs during the summer. We lived in a village on the plains, and for us, summer was magical; it meant good weather, long days, beautiful green foliage, and plenty of food, especially fruit. On the morning of *Tishebov*, the men went to the synagogue to read the laments, the *Eycho,* the *Kines*. The women didn't go, but came to our house instead. We had a porch big enough to hold a large group of people and it provided shelter from the sun throughout the day. The women arrived early in the morning, sat around in a circle on chairs while we, the smaller girls, mostly sat on the ground. When everyone had arrived, they began to read the *Kines*. They read it like the men did in the synagogue, dividing the verses among them. Those who did not know the melody read only the words—everyone participated in the way she could."

"When it was over, we had nothing to do for the rest of the day, since *Tishebov* is a holiday and it is forbidden to work. And since it is also a fast day, there was no need to prepare food and to serve or wash dishes either. So for the women, it was a real holiday, even more than other holidays, when, even if one tried to prepare everything the day before, there was always some anxiety over the food. The *Kines* are not long, and after we had finished we still had the whole day to ourselves. Since there was nothing to do, the women talked and told stories. There was a wonderful … a special atmosphere. *Tishebov* is a day of mourning, so the talking was calm and intimate. There were no arguments or quarrels, and no business was discussed. But the atmosphere was not sad. The women told all kinds of stories, even humorous ones. This is how we spent the day, enjoying the shade, the good weather, the stories, and the fact that we were together."

"It's hard for me to get used to this new life. I know it won't last long. My disease has its pace and it's impossible to stop. When I was no longer able to go to the synagogue, those clever men at the rabbinate appointed another president. They said that a handicapped person should not direct a congregation. But it was only my body that was sick; my mind was as sharp as ever. Our people simply ignored the decision, pretending not to know about it. Since then, they have started coming to my home every Shabes after the service to discuss the matters of the community and decide what to do—exactly as we had done before. I did not ask this from anyone and would have agreed to being replaced. But they are wonderful people, my friends. I am grateful, very grateful to them! And also to you, Juditka, for coming, even though it's far … coming on Shabes and visiting me during the short time you spend in Pest."

"You see, first I got used to the idea that I wouldn't travel any more. Then that

I wouldn't be able to go to town, then that my world would be only a short walk from home, across the park to the synagogue. Finally, I accepted that the world was this apartment. Now, I cannot even stand up any more. I have what I see from my bed. So now the world comes to me—you wonderful people come to me. Still, I wish it were me going out into the world…"

The woman who sat next to me in the Kazinczy Street synagogue (1979)

"My husband is right not to let you record his prayers. Who knows what you are after! I know your kind. You will put these things on a record, get a lot of money for it and then not care any more. People will buy it and do what they want with it. They will laugh at us, ridicule us."

The man who always sat apart with his chair pulled up to the wall (1978–1980)

"It is impossible to record prayer. Because *kavunes*, which is the only important thing, happens in the present. You don't graduate from it. You can never say: now I've learned this, I've done my job and can go on to something else."

"In order to be in the prayer, you have to forget about time … and all the things in your life…"

"And when it is not like this, when, for example, a cantor doesn't sing with *kavunes*, when he does not bring out the sound of the word, the details and thoughts within them … the essence … that is painful to listen to. I would like to scream, it hurts my ears—it's physical pain for me."

"When you pray, sincerely and from the heart, you don't care what the others think of you. But when you make a recording, you labor to get some … document, something for others to listen to, a thing that remains and that does not change, and therefore it is not … alive."

"I wouldn't want to hear my father's voice coming from a tape. What would I not give to have him here, praying with me, and to hear my mother sing her songs! But to listen to their voices on tape … dead people's voices! The thought of it sends shivers down my spine. Their voices are in my heart. You can hear them in my prayer, and when I die, they will die with me. And this is how it should be."

"When I die, someone will remember something of my prayer, and this will perhaps contain the voice of my father—but you will never be able to sort these things out. You scholars want to know how things are exactly—what was there before and what each person took from it and added to it, for instance, whether the man you are recording remembers the melodies of his father. Well, I can tell you he does not. What do you want from the past? Listen to the people who are around you in this life."

"If you are moved by the living, the dead will speak to you. You don't have to make any special effort. It's enough to listen, to be present … be with us … with those few who still know how to pray…"

György Kármán, organist of the prayer house in the Rabbinical Seminary (2001–2008)

"You don't hear that kind of service any more. It's difficult to believe such a thing could happen … for the rabbi to ban the organ from our prayer house. For me personally, it doesn't matter, I wanted to retire anyway. But in my view, it's a big mistake. Our services at the Rabbinical Seminary were special. The organ compositions, the songs and the pieces for the choir created an ambiance you could not find anywhere else. It was a wonderful atmosphere, warm and welcoming. People felt they were part of a family. Our prayer house was always packed—even during Communist times and ever since. According to the new rabbi, an organ and a choir do not belong to the Jewish tradition. Of course, his decision had nothing to do with tradition; it was pure politics. In the present politicized climate of religious life, he had no choice."

"As to tradition—the organ and choir have been part of the Jewish tradition for more than two hundred years! And this particular prayer house was originally built for services with an organ and a choir—it was designed with a special space on the balcony for the organ and the choir. To destroy this, to pretend that this two-hundred-year history never happened, to erase the differences among the different Jewish services… This new passion, a creed almost, that proclaims the existence of one single 'correct' and 'authentic' way of prayer and mold everything into a rigid homogenous mass like an army… It's sad, very sad!"

"For me, this *is* the Jewish tradition. I was raised with this kind of service from early childhood. In Szeged, where I come from, there was a large Neolog community—Neolog in the best sense of the word. It meant that we were deeply religious but also modern. We kept all the fast days; I keep them even today, not only Yom Kippur and *Tishebov* but also the smaller ones, the fasts of Gedalya and Esther. We ate kosher and there were separate dishes for Pesach. Working on Shabes was out of the question. On Shabes, we walked to the synagogue and in the afternoon we studied the texts. My father taught us; he translated the texts and explained the meaning of the words. But we were also educated in Hungarian and German literature, and at home we spoke both languages. I played piano and studied mathematics and all the other secular subjects."

"In Szeged, there was a large Neolog community with two synagogues: one large and one small—the smaller one held only a few hundred people. Both were packed on Shabes and holidays. For me, Shabos meant those beautiful choral and organ pieces. We loved those compositions, and used to sing them at home as well. In the large synagogue, there was always a big crowd on Shabos—people came from all over the country to hear our rabbi, the famous Immanuel Löw. You think preaching does not belong in the service. But it depends who does it. The way Löw spoke! I remember his famous speech in 1943 when—in front of thousands of people—he cursed Hitler and fascism. He was imprisoned during the Horthy era."

"There was an Orthodox prayer house not far from our synagogue. But those were different times: they did what they did and it would have never occurred to us to force them to pray according to our style, and they also left us alone with our service. During *Sukkaus*, on *Simchas Tauro*, I went over with the other children to see them dancing and hear their songs because that was special, something we did not have in our synagogue."

"And every year, there was one occasion when they helped us out. During the High Holidays, there is a blessing said for the entire community by the *kohanim*, and this blessing is very important. It's for the whole year and for all of us. Rabbi Löw wanted to make sure that this blessing was said by *kohanim* who kept all the commandments down to the smallest details. And since our community was liberal and he was too polite to inquire, let alone check, who kept what, he thought it better to ask the *kohanim* from the Orthodox community to perform this task. He asked them to send the same *kohanim* who blessed their community to bless us as well. So these *kohanim* from that very Orthodox community left in the middle of their service, came over, blessed us, and then went back to continue the prayer in their *shul*."

"You would think that such ultra-Orthodox Jews would never set foot in a synagogue that had organ music and a women's choir during the High Holidays because, according to them, these are things strictly forbidden. But this was not the case. They were happy to come and felt honored to have been asked. They thought it was their responsibility—a good deed, a *mitsve*—to bless our congregation."

György Kroó ("Gyuri," chairman of the Department of Musicology and director of the Music Division of the Hungarian Radio, 1979)

"You won't find it. The music of the Jews before the war—you won't find it."

"I remember our congregation in my hometown before the war, before the labor camp, when I was still a child. I don't speak about this to anyone today ... not within the walls of this Radio building and not outside it. Everyone was different in that congregation and everyone prayed differently. Over the years, we got used to each person's craziness. There was Uncle Shoma with his continual gossiping and endless, boring stories, Uncle Benő, who always came late but then prayed with such devotion that he had to scream sometimes, then, there was ... Uncle this and Uncle that ... never mind, the names wouldn't mean anything to you. There was even a Hasid. I remember him well; he came to our *shul* in his kaftan and *shtreiml*, something I had never seen before. Our community was not Hassidic and not even properly Orthodox, but in spite of that, he prayed with us. And our congregation was what it was because he was there, too. The community was not like this or that person. You could not tell what a typical member of our congregation looked like and how a typical prayer sounded. The congregation was all of us—these extremes ... sometimes shocking, almost ridiculous, extremes and differences—together. And that you will never be able to understand."

"I hope this place is not bugged ... because I need to speak to you also about something else. You should be aware that ... how shall I put it ... you should know that if you continue this thing ... going from one prayer house to the other, with your tape recorder, then you should better get out of the country sooner or later. In fact, rather sooner … as soon as possible. If something happens to you, if you get into trouble, I won't be able to help. I'm a little cog in the system."

"But where should one go? I don't know. I really don't know… Israel? They have a flag, an anthem and an army, and so they are a nation. Is it really that easy—a flag and an anthem and then you have a home? On the other hand, to stay here and be Jewish in secret … that's no good either. I don't know… I don't know…"

"Emil" (Emil Goitein, Elkono Sholoim ben Kleinemus, 1990–1998)

"What do you want from me, my dear? Why do you come on Thursday when, you should know by now, I am the commander of a sinking ship? Unless I organize it, we won't have a *minyen* for Shabes. During winter, we get it together somehow, but summer is difficult. One person is on vacation at Lake Balaton, the other is in the hospital; one cannot come because it's too hot, the other has relatives over from Australia, and so on. So excuse me if I'm not quite with it today; my head is elsewhere."

"But first let me close the window, it's impossible to talk with this noise. When my parents moved in here, this was considered a most desirable location: the upper floor of a building with a salon facing the grand boulevard. In those days, there were horse carriages and you could leave the window open the whole day. Now you get suffocated by traffic fumes, and have to put up with dreadful honking and drilling the whole day. As far as I can remember, this was my home, first with my parents, brothers and sisters, then, after the war, with my mother, and later, after she had died and I had married, Ilonka moved in with me. By the way, you should taste this pastry. Ilonka baked it especially for you. In my opinion, though I might be biased, she bakes the best kosher pastries in town."

"You should have seen me twenty years ago, executive director of a company! And what a company! With us, the special thing was that those who wanted to keep the rules of the religion did not have to work on Shabes and holidays. They made up for the lost hours with overtime on other days. I was the director and so I gave permission—I had the power to do it. And everyone worked extra hard and with great enthusiasm because they knew that if this company collapsed, they would not find another job that would allow them to live like Jews."

"It was a gigantic and immensely successful company. We had branches all over the country and did business with the West, in fact, excellent business—and all this in Communist times! There was a crisis every day; it cannot be otherwise with such a big enterprise. But I was always calm. I never lost sleep over those things. I knew I would find a solution in the end. But this business with the *shul*, the anxiety I have getting ten people together—I am already nervous days before Shabes."

"Perhaps it is time to close up shop … to give up this community. The Kazinczy synagogue is around the corner; we could merge with them. I often tell myself what a stubborn donkey I am to go through this every week. But I know that as long as have the strength to move, I will continue to do it. In the Rumbach Street synagogue, where I was brought up, we had a special *nusach*. It was traditional and precise and simple, but it had its special color. All of us who are now at the Sip Street prayer house are originally Rumbach people; all of us learned to pray there before the war. Today, only a few old people remember the Rumbach *nusach*.

"Because it is one thing to pray, and another to pray in a congregation that's really yours. When I lead the service in another *shul*, I am completely exhausted afterwards—after all, I am no longer young. It's different with my community, with the Rumbach people. It's enough for me to pray softly, almost as if I would when I am alone at home. I hum the first line, and the voices behind me join in immediately. We have the same pace, the same volume, feeling and *nusach*. Nobody runs ahead or pulls back, and even if every now and then someone has an urge to show off, it remains within the calm and intimate atmosphere of our style. It takes no energy to lead them. I don't have to do anything, I just let it happen."

"Now, my dear Juditka, let me tell you something. The problem with you is that, although you know this and that, you lack the basis. By the way, I have seen worse. There is this young fellow, a perfectly nice boy—nothing wrong with him except that he's a cantor. He knows nothing and everyone loves him. That's how things are these days. He is already a cantor in the big synagogue and he does not have the slightest idea what it means to *daven*. He sings tunes. He sings notes: one nice note, and then another nice note, like in the opera. Now, as you know, I love opera, especially Mozart and Wagner. But one should sing differently in the synagogue."

"When I was young, cantors meant everything to me. Back then we had no money for concerts or opera. For us, music was the band of the fire brigade in the park and the cantor in the synagogue. Some boys in the Rumbach synagogue, who, like me, were dying to hear good cantors, got together and made a plan. On Shabes, when the Torah reading was over at Rumbach Street, we went to Dohány Street to hear their cantor. We calculated when *musaf* would start in the Kazinczy Street *shul* because we wanted to hear their cantor also. So when we had enough of the cantor at Dohány, we went to Kazinczy. Often, as we were going from one synagogue to the other, we would meet another group of boys making the same rounds—but they would start at Kazinczy, be on their way to Dohány, and then to Rumbach. This was our joy on Shabes, this was our opera."

"Izrael Tkatsch's singing was unforgettable. He was what I believe a *chazzn* should be: a true *zoger chazzn*. There are different types of cantors; the *zoger* is the one who *says* the prayer. A true *zoger* cantor, even if he embellishes the melody, because all cantors do that, puts the emphasis on the text. He does not *sing*, he recites … declaims. He cares for the clear pronunciation of the words. But what matters even more is that the congregation is able to feel from his declamation the essence of the prayers."

"Today there are no such cantors; the whole art has declined. I hear beautiful voices, wonderful technique; just a few days ago, here in the Dohány Street synagogue, someone sang a high E in a clear, brilliant voice. But all this means nothing to me; it does not speak to me. For me, the simple recitative of Tkatsch meant more. That moved me. His voice came from within, from the depth of his heart. It spoke to you; it was warm and pleading and humble, and at the same time firm and secure and clean."

"What I would not give to be able to sing like that! To be a cantor! It's a real art, the only art we have in the synagogue. But in the end, it doesn't really matter. What matters is *davenen* and *nusach*, to be moved by the words and sing them with the proper melody. Only if these things are in place can one begin with fantasies. I confess that I mix a bit of this and that into the *nusach*. I even use melodies from operas. Here is this motive from the aria of … what's his name, help me, I am forgetting everything... Ah yes, Beckmesser, that motive from his aria, it's in Wagner's *Meistersinger*, you know. I discovered that it fits the notes of the *nusach* of this prayer perfectly. It's an accident, of course. When I recite the prayer and come to this motive, I make a little insertion, which is my invention and fits perfectly, and only I know where it comes from."

"So, to come back to our main point, the problem with you is … by the way, turn off the tape recorder, for your own sake, because you're not going to be proud of what I am about to say. In any case, I am telling you these things only because we are related—distantly, it's true—but still, I am something of an uncle to you. If you were not my family, I would not dare say a word about these things, but with you I can be honest."

"The problem with you, my dear Juditka, is that you don't pray. You should *daven* your prayers every day without fail, and at least on holidays, with their melody. Then, in time, you will realize that this whole thing is not such a big deal to learn and the rhythm is not complicated at all. You'll learn it without even noticing. And by the time you are as old and senile as I am, you won't even remember what could have possibly been difficult about it. But if you don't pray! Then there is nothing to explain. One learns to pray only by praying. But if you don't want to pray, then why learn how to do it?"

"When I was in the labor camp… I hope the tape recorder is off, because when people hear this, they won't believe it. But it does not matter any more…"

"So to come back to our story, when I was in the labor camp, I ate kosher the whole time. Now, eating kosher meant that I ate almost nothing. And sometimes, I did not drink the tea they gave us, because the cup was not clean enough for me."

"I kept my prayer shawl; it was with me all the time. In the concentration camps they took everything, but in the labor camp you could have personal objects. I got up an hour before everybody else every day. Imagine: we had to get up at five, in the winter, and I would get up at four to recite my prayers. I went outside, put the prayer shawl around my head, my body, and began to pray. And then, well then … I was in another world. I was no longer in the camp; I was somewhere else... The prayer shawl around me, the sound of my own prayer… It went on like this every day."

"If I think of this today, I do not understand. It made no sense; it was insane under those circumstances. And if you ask me why I did it, I cannot answer. There is no explanation..."

"Only Woods"

"Hari" (Avrohom Tzvi Erbst, 2001–2008)

"I will tell you about my life, but I have one condition: that you won't ask about the deportation and Auschwitz and all the rest."

"I was born in a village so small that it is not even on the map. It is called Barnabás. I always tell people that I am from Raho, which was a nearby settlement. When I say that I am from Raho, people may know what I am talking about, but no one seems to have heard of Barnabás. It was a very small place indeed, a miserable Ruthenian village with a few Jewish families—we were all relatives."

"There was nothing in that village, absolutely nothing, only woods and woods, and all around, woods. And bears. And wolves … sometimes the wolves came to our house. Of course, there was no electricity or running water. Not a single newspaper, book, radio, or musical instrument. Things like theaters, concerts, and museums—we had never even heard of them!"

"We were so poor that as I am telling you about it now, I can hardly believe it was true. We were always hungry, and it was only on holidays that we might have had meat, if at all. My mother baked bread for Shabes, and after Shabes we sliced it up and everyone had his portion for the week. A few weeks before Pesach, we began collecting. Wherever we went we looked for food. If we found a carrot or a potato in the fields somewhere, we put it away. We did this for weeks, so that by Pesach, we had a nice collection. We baked *matsa* in the village, every year at another house where there was an oven, and made wine from raisins. We also got help from a wealthy Jew who had taken it upon himself to help the poor Jews of the area. We got vinegar from him."

"There was no synagogue, we prayed in someone's house, one year here, the other year there, but mostly at our home. But we had a *baltfile*; his name was Uncle Adler. I remember only vaguely how he sang, but I know that as a child I liked it very much. We had prayer books, although often we had to share, and sometimes it was just a collection of loose pages of what was once a book. A relative of mine knew some of the *zmires*, and I remember vaguely that the older boys had gatherings where they sang Yiddish songs—they brought them from the city."

"But we rarely sang because we were hungry, even on Shabes—who would want to sing on an empty stomach? *Moytsei* Shabes … that we would have fun after the Shabes ended … It's a modern invention, such things did not exist in my time. The moment Shabes was over, we began to work—bringing water from the well, washing dishes, preparing for the next day. It was such a miserable life, so much suffering! I do not like to remember it."

"As children, we were already looking for work. Most of the work in the region had to do with wood, since that was all there was. I started out working for a lumber company. I would carry logs with my friend, another child like myself. A group of men cut the trees. The trunks were cut into logs, slid down the slope of the mountain and then chopped into even smaller pieces. The bigger ones were tied together into rafts and sent downriver on the Tisza. That was the method of transportation in the wood business. A few men would stand on the rafts, making sure the wood arrived at its destination. This was very dangerous: sometimes the rope got torn, the logs parted, and the raft fell apart and the people standing on it fell into the river. And if this happened when the Tisza was flooding, it was impossible to swim back to shore. Several men died in this way."

"The sawing produced a lot of sawdust. There were always mountains of it in the forest, wherever the work was going on. Sawdust burns easily and fast. When it accumulated, it was piled into a heap and set on fire. The heap burned slowly from top to bottom. This was a treacherous business, because sometimes the fire would spread and you could not see which part of the heap was burning. I don't understand exactly how this happens—it's like a corridor of fire running under a thin layer of sawdust that is not burning; you cannot see anything on the surface. We were carrying logs toward the edge of the heap, which was supposed to be safe since the fire was on the top of the heap, in the

middle. But once, my friend stepped onto a spot that had been burnt out underneath and fell into a flaming pit. I pulled him out and we ran to the river, but by then he was burned pretty badly. When the workers found out, they threw us out immediately. They said we weren't mature enough for the job."

"I had to look for another job. My second job was to clean the forest paths; I also did this together with another boy. We had to pick up the smaller logs and debris, take it off the path. We left the village early in the morning, walked in the forest all day long and had no food apart from a slice of bread that we had brought from home. When we got home, it was already sunset and we were starving. On good days, there was warm food at home, perhaps cooked peas. Later, at the yeshiva, I had "eating days." That was the system in those days; the students ate with a different family each day. I cannot recall what kind of food we ate there, but I remember that we had a cup of coffee every morning and that it was very good."

"My father was a wonderful, special person. I have a painting of him; a friend of mine painted it after a photograph. It's quite a good painting—indeed, this is what he looked like, with that characteristic expression on his face, as if he were about to invite you to his house. He opened a shop—not a particularly good idea for a man like him! People in the village were poor and could not pay. They asked my father to give them the goods on credit. Of course, my father did not have the heart to say no. They kept coming and never paid, because they were indeed very poor. It did not take long for my father to go bankrupt."

"He was a goodhearted man, optimistic and full of laughter. Whenever he saw someone passing through the village, he invited him over to our house and made him stay for supper. This was funny, because there was hardly anything to eat—but he made him sit with us anyway and struck up a conversation. He simply loved people. So in the end, he found himself a job as a notary and helped people in our village with their problems—for they were a very backward crowd, most people could not read and write. He was eighty-six when they put him on the train…"

"My mother? I don't know… There were twenty years between them; it was my father's second marriage. She bore eight children within a very short period—four boys and four girls. And all the time, even when she was pregnant, she would work from dawn to late at night. There was a small shop about six or eight kilometers from the village; she would carry things home from there. We used water from the Tisza for washing, but did not drink it. There was a well at the train station, about half a kilometer away; we carried water from there. We had a cow, which she milked every morning—or at least tried, because it did not give much milk. But once, no … perhaps twice, we even had a calf! We helped my mother with this and that—my father, the children and

especially the girls, since they worked mostly at home sewing clothes for the Ruthenian peasant women in the village. But since we all worked, we did not have much time either. And my brothers and I came home practically only to eat in the evening and for Shabes; otherwise we were at school or working."

"I did not know my mother. I had no idea what she was thinking and what kind of person she was. We never talked; there was no time. I think she was in a state of shock from the moment this life—motherhood and the unbelievable amount of work it involved—began for her. She did not have a single moment to herself … always children and housework … it was inhuman … that life killed everything in her … it killed her."

"The public school was in another village, about a kilometer and a half away, and in winter, the snow was often half a meter high. But in summer, there was a bicycle. I had a cousin who lived in a nearby village who had a bicycle and taught me how to ride. In summer, he let me use his bicycle. Well, not too often, about once a month. The elementary school was Ruthenian—one class for all ages. Amongst ourselves we spoke Yiddish, but we also knew Ruthenian, because that was the language of the village. I have absolutely no recollection of what we learned—if we learned anything at all at that school. The only thing that stayed with me is the Ruthenian national hymn and some national poems; we repeated those all the time. We also had *cheider*, but not regularly because the Jews in our village couldn't afford to hire a teacher every year. We would teach each other. We tried to learn things on our own, so that at least we understood the words of the prayers."

"The good things? The forest and the birds. Wherever you looked, there were woods and woods—endless stretches of woods. But the most beautiful thing was the Tisza. I had an uncle who lived near us on the other side of the river. My brothers and I would go over to him on Shabes afternoons; he taught us Torah and Talmud. When he was young, he had a bee farm. I don't think it was ever a big business, but by the time I got to know him he was very old and only had a few beehives and occasionally a few jars of honey. If we prepared the Torah section well, he would give us … oh, I can't continue, I have to laugh … what do you think he gave us? Not chocolate or pastry. A cup of water—with a drop of honey in it. Yes, a cup of water with one drop of honey!"

"But I wanted to tell you something else in connection with this: there were two bridges over the Tisza, the railway bridge and the wooden bridge. To get to my uncle's farm, we crossed the wooden bridge—and that road was beautiful. It led through meadows full of flowers. All around and also along the riverbank there were flowers of all imaginable colors, and from the bridge you could see the fish swimming in the water. It was breathtakingly perfect and peaceful. To this day, whenever I have a good dream, this is the image I see: colorful flowers on the bank of a river and fish swimming."

"*Tishebov* was special. In summer, the woods were filled with raspberries—those big and sweet raspberries that grow only in the forest of high mountains. During the week, we did not have time to go to the forest, and besides, it would have been dangerous to go there alone. Early in the morning on *Tishebov*, we got together and read the *echo*, but since it's not very long, we were free the rest of the day, and *Tishebov* is a holiday so we were not allowed to work. So what did we do? We went to the forest—the whole family, that is, all the Jews of the village—with big baskets, and picked raspberries. Two of us would stand at the edge of the group and beat buckets to frighten the bears away—of course the bears would have loved to participate, since they also like raspberries. It was a superb idea to do this on *Tishebov*, because it was a fast day and we could not eat, so we took the whole harvest home."

"During my childhood, I left the village only once. We travelled to the wedding of some relative. That was the first time I heard an instrument—until then, I did not even know such a thing existed. The musicians were Ruthenians: violin, cimbalom and bass. Before the wedding I asked one of my sisters to teach me to dance. She taught me to dance the tango."

"How my father found the money to send me to yeshiva, I don't know. At any rate, after I finished the four years of elementary school, he sent me off with a little money and a letter to a place that today is in Romania. But I did not spend much time there, because the war broke out and then came the deportation, Auschwitz and Mauthausen—but we agreed not to talk about that."

"When the American troops reached Mauthausen, I was too weak even to sit up. Somehow, I made it to Budapest. It wasn't so simple, of course. I did not come directly, but went back to my village first to see whether anyone had returned. Then, because there was nowhere to go, people advised me to go to Budapest. By that time I was in a terrible state. My body simply did not function: one organ was not working, another damaged, another infected. I could barely hold myself up."

"After the war, the Joint set up hospitals and sanatoriums for Jews who had returned from the camps. Thanks to them, I was admitted to a hospital. For the next six years, I was sent back and forth between hospitals and sanatoriums; I was such a wreck that the doctors did not know what to do with me."

"You would think that after what had happened, Jews would be helping each other. Nothing of the sort happened. The rich Jews stuck together and grabbed what they could. I had no relatives in Budapest, so I was sent to the hospital in Debrecen and put in the basement. It's true, I was not the only one in the basement; in that situation, after the war, the hospitals did not have enough space for beds. But most of the patients had a relative or a friend who brought them fruit and vegetables, and also clothes when needed. I was not from that area, not even from Hungary, and I had lost everybody. I barely spoke Hungarian in those days, so in their eyes, I was nobody. There was not one of them who would have shared anything with me."

"Somehow I managed to get to the sanatorium in Mátrafüred, and things got better. The sanatorium was an entirely new experience for me. There were patients from Budapest, many of whom were cultured and discussed all kinds of cultural matters. This was the first time I heard of theater and music. Imagine how I felt, a total ignoramus. I did not have the slightest idea what they were talking about. These cultured Jews were, in fact, quite a nasty crowd. They were snobs and looked down on everybody who was less educated than they were. I could tell stories! Every morning, I put on my *tfilin*, covered my head with the *talis* and began to say my prayers. And what did they do? They laughed at me and made fun of me. They called me a 'bigot' and a *polishi*, which meant something like 'ignorant peasant'; this is what they called us poor Jews who came to Hungary from the East, from Ukraine, Galicia, and Poland."

"But some of them did not laugh, and were actually nice and willing to help. One of these was Gyuri, who, as you know, later made a big career for himself. He deserved it, for he already knew a lot back then, even before he started studying at the Academy of Music. He had lost his family and was completely alone. All he had was a violin that he kept under his bed. He played almost every day and explained things to me, so that by the time I got out of the sanatorium I knew about composers and had listened to some music. Later, when he held a high position at the Radio and was a professor at the Academy of Music, he always made sure I got a ticket for good concerts. In return, I brought him *tsibere* for Pesach. It's a shame he died so young."

"When I got out of the sanatorium, I had no idea what to do with myself. The little knowledge I had related to wood—not very practical in a big city. I knew nobody in Budapest, had no money, and could not imagine what I was going to do and even where to put my head down. Fortunately, someone took me in and let me share his rented room for a while. Gradually, I began to function on my own. This all happened by chance, because here and there I met people who were nice to me and helped me learn things—although, to tell you the truth, this did not happen very often. Slowly, I worked myself into electronics, took some courses and began to look for work. I was offered a minor temporary job at the Central Research Institute for Physics. It was originally for a year, but soon I became a technical assistant at the cosmic radiation department—almost without any formal training. I retired from that department with numerous awards after forty years of work."

"At the sanatorium, I was sometimes asked to serve as *baltfile*. Not that I knew the melodies very well, but at least I knew the texts of the prayers. I did whatever I could using the melodies as I remembered them from home and my studies at the yeshiva. I was lucky, because the person who took me in at the beginning also took me to his *shul* on Vörösmarty Street."

"I learned a lot there. The congregation came from all over Hungary and the surrounding countries. There were a few older men who knew almost everything there was to know about the prayers. I cannot tell you where they came from—I probably knew at the time, but after a while it became irrelevant. They drew my attention to details I had not considered before. We were a strong but very humble community; we all knew something, and we taught each other. We took the prayer seriously and did not want anything beyond that. There were no ranks, which is how it should be. In a real Jewish community, there are no chief rabbis or chief cantors or such ridiculous things.

As a result, we never asked for support from the rabbinate. We preferred to be left alone in our simple ways. Most of those still around today and who can pray properly, started out at this community. For instance, it was where I got to know Marci, and so it was easy for us to coordinate the roles later, when we served at the Hunyadi Square synagogue together."

"I want to show you a photograph, a historic photograph. It was taken at *Simhas tayre* in 1982, at the Vörösmarty *shul*; you have probably seen it, because Marci also has a copy and is very fond of it. Marci is on the left, holding the Torah; next to him is Henrik Steinberg, and this is me, holding the prayer book. The person on the far right is a certain Gergely, whose family name I cannot recall. I know his Jewish name; for me, the Jewish names are always easier to remember because of the many blessings, the *misheberach*, I said for them; he was called Eliyahu Nussen ben Yakov. He came from Nyirbátor and had a grocery store. Steinberg's name was Hayim ben Yoseys Sender Halevi. He was the *rashekol* and also the *baltfile*—a man with great knowledge. His wife, Sárika—Shura bas Nehemia—is still alive; she must be in her nineties, but is still entirely fresh in spirit. You should visit her once. She would be able to tell you very interesting things about those times."

"But even at a place like the Vörösmarty and only a few years after the war, the rich separated themselves from the poor. Most of them were doing surprisingly well, at least by those days' standards, but pretended not to notice the desperate situation some us were in. On Shabes, hot food was served after the service; the well-to-do members of the community got the money together, and naturally—though I never contributed—I ate with them. But that was all, their generosity ended there. I have memories so unbelievable, so absurd and embarrassing that I am ashamed to recount them even now."

"How much misery one had to live through! But there were also good things in those days. I began to go to the opera and concerts. A friend of mine figured out how to get cheap opera tickets—that is, for even less than the normal price, since tickets were cheap anyway. But we had no money and every penny mattered. The only problem was that you had to stand in line the night before in order to get these super cheap tickets, and we all had to go to work early in the morning. So we took turns and bought the tickets for each other. I fell in love with opera. Later I began to go to concerts, and they made an even deeper impression on me."

"Music was a revelation for me. There was a period when concerts were the most important thing in my life. It went like this: during the day—work, in the evening—concert, and in the morning, on Shabes and holidays—prayer. Early in the morning, travelling on the bus to the prayer house, I would hold on to my prayer book wrapped in the pages of a newspaper. The thought that soon I would *daven*—even the thought gave me strength for the whole day. And in the evening: concert! Because Gyuri helped me with tickets, I could get in even when a celebrity came and the prices were higher, or when it was sold out. This was sometimes funny, because those snob VIPs from the Research Institute were sure that a *polishi* like me never listened to music. Then they would see me sitting in the best seat at the most exclusive concert. I can assure you that I knew more about the pieces on the program than they did."

"Sometimes, I ask myself what would have happened if I had emigrated. This was, of course, out of the question, because at the time when one could still cross the border, I was in such a physical state that I could hardly walk to the end of the corridor of the hospital. Perhaps I would have made more money and it would have been easier with the religion. But one thing is certain: I would not have been able to go to concerts three times a week. And that was my great luck, an amazing gift—to be able to educate myself and learn to love music."

"Nowadays, I do not go to concerts as much as I used to. As I get older, it becomes harder and harder to get to town from Buda. It's a beautiful place and I like to live there, but it's far from everything. Getting to the Hunyadi synagogue was already hard enough. Some years ago, Szepesi asked me to pray with them at the Károlyi Square *kihle* because he could no longer do the services alone. That's an even longer trip. I don't mind, because it's a lovely community, but, at my age, to travel an hour and a half on Shabes and then sing through the entire service alone is too much. Things were different when Szepesi was still alive. And now Feigele is also sick ... very sick."

"I am grateful to the Almighty for giving me these years and the strength to lead this community and take care of the people. When I stand in front of the congregation and pray—I stand with my back to them, of course, and still I feel exactly what they need. I cannot pray for them, but I try to help with the tempo and style, do what is best for

them. At the same time, I am alone with myself, and ultimately … before Him. It is not easy to be in this place—to do what the congregation expects from you and at the same time remain yourself. But I am happy to do it because I love this community. I have come to know each of them well, and we joke a lot. If I don't, who else would help them?"

"But it's a whole different thing to pray alone. If I am not leading the service, I never stand in the first row, where one is visible. I want to be left alone. In the old days, I used to go to the Kazinczy Street synagogue and I knew Moshe Weiss, who was a charismatic and spiritual man. He saw that I was serious and asked me to stand in the first row. He wanted to have a circle of knowledgeable men around him so that he would not feel left in a void during the prayer. I felt honored—but did not want to. If you stand in the spotlight, so to speak, and especially in such a big synagogue … then it's not the same. The prayer does not flow the same way. But he was persistent and asked again. So I opened the prayer book and read him the line '*Adoishem* is near to all who call, to all who call in truth.' He smiled, and from then on he left me alone. He understood perfectly what I meant. Because this is how it is: *the more you seem to be on the margin, invisible, the better you can concentrate on the important things.*"

"But even when I am praying for the community, I pray, as they say, 'from the heart.' You told me the other day that after you transcribed the melodies of my prayer, you

discovered that I *daven* differently every time. I never noticed. To prepare the melody ahead of time, think about the motives and have a plan—that's impossible. Of course, with a text that is recited only once a year, like *Akdomus*, for instance, I think about the melody and try it out at home in order to be able to properly match the text and the melody. For Shabes this is not necessary. But when I pray, whichever prayer it might be, I don't think of the melody any more. I look at the words, read them, concentrate and don't care what comes out."

"You asked me whether music, that is, the real music we listen to in concert halls, influences my prayer. Well, that is out of the question. I never use anything from that music in the prayer. It wouldn't cross my mind. These are two completely different things. One is the music of enjoyment, and it is beautiful for that reason. I know that some religious people would disagree, but I am convinced that this music also comes from the Almighty. It must, because it moves us so deeply—pieces like Beethoven's G major Piano Concerto for instance. But prayer is not enjoyment. It is *kavunes*. What matters is the intensity with which you live through the words."

"It is not difficult to read the text, and it is not difficult to sing these melodies. What is difficult, indeed terribly difficult, is *concentration*: to live through, with all your might, the meaning of every word."

"Before I go to the front to pray, I often say to my friends in the first row: 'Please hold me down if you see that I am getting carried away, if I start throwing my hands up in the air, and so on.' I am afraid that one day I will get a heart attack. But I could not do it any other way."

"And this is the reason I do not want the video, which we filmed the other day, be shown to anyone. It was not shot on Shabes, from that point of view it is all right, but I do not want people to see me cry. I am not ashamed of crying. But people will misunderstand; they will think that I am crying because I am moved. They will think that this is about emotions, about sad memories and other painful things. But this is not the case at all. The tears came because of the intensity—because I was close to the words. One makes an enormous effort to be at the right place, within the words, to the point that your mind almost bursts with concentration—and then the tears begin to flow. Those who do not live in this world won't understand. It is better to keep it to ourselves."

"There is a saying: 'Know where you come from, know where you are going, and know in front of whom you stand with your deeds.' I hope that I never forget in front of whom I stand when I pray and at all times, and that is the essence. But this is not the only important thing. And it is not so easy to say where I come from. My roots are not only Jewish. They are also Hungarian: this culture and this society and this city, and this particular community that puts its faith in me."

"When you speak about me, tell people where I came from. My whole education was four years of elementary school. And what an elementary school, what a backward region, what a level! Tell them from what depths I rose to where I find myself today. But all this is not important. At heart I am still a *polishi*."

III. Shards and Flowers

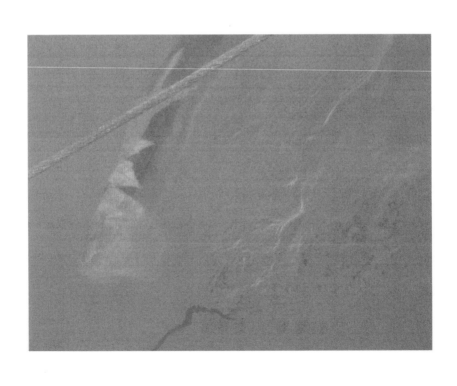

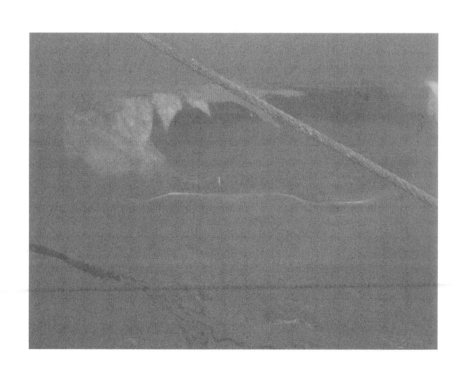

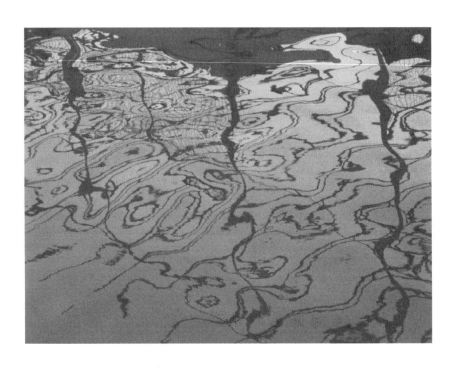

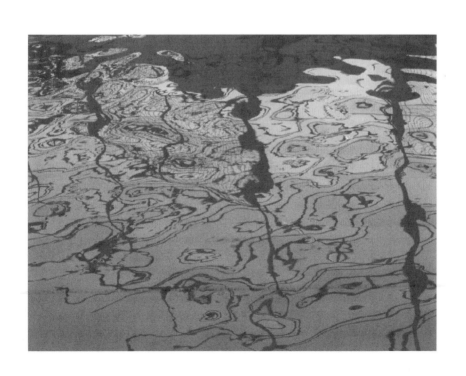

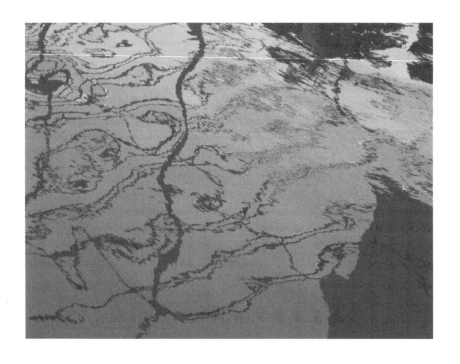

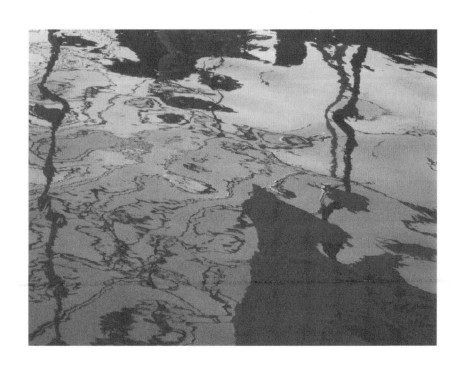

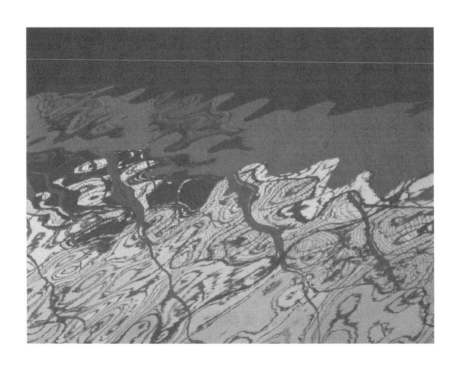

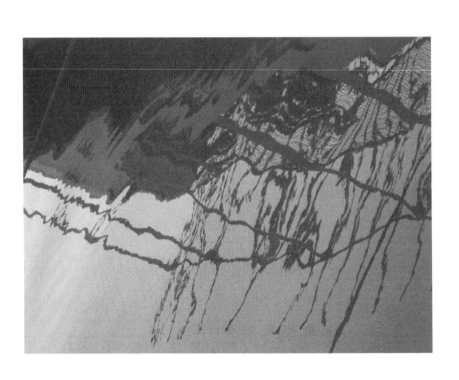

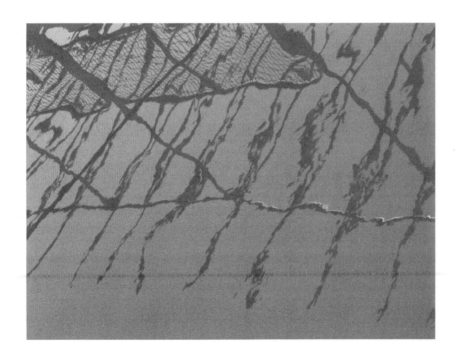

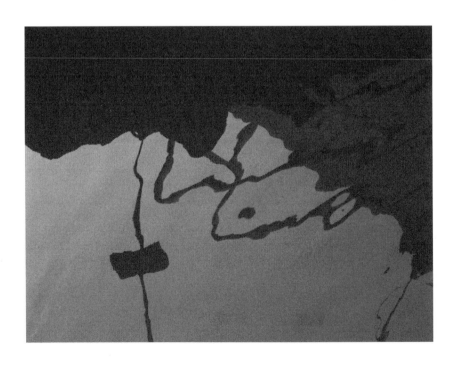

It's A Tape

In memory of those who did not come back

ashen trails on magnetic tape
scars on the face of remembrance
a systematized, complete and collected
opus magnum

he did not look at me while informing
as is it written in the book:

"My first informant was an old man
who refused to tell me his name"

and after he had left I faced myself
gulped by darkness

and ever and ever it grows and swells
the there-isn't-any-trace

tracing after myself among the typed
the scanned, the notes, the classified

among them

the microphone's velvet profundity
shudders, without me, I am no longer

I steal my way out, slip through the cracks
of the measured multitudes of silences

I dream of shards

it's because of the smoke that my hands
are always cold when I rise to them

the wind blew it upward, the magnetic dust
from our path, and now the sound of breaking glass

someone enters, the noise of steps
on the tape and my voice

these are only fragments that will be corrected
into a coherent and scholarly

but for now I keep on talking to myself
about how I don't know whether he is still alive

he survived it all, perhaps he'll survive this as well
my silence stretched above the passing of time

outside before my eyes a tree-branch
breaks and a rift in the snowfall

I pull my chair into the corner and listen
how splinters of torn chords
float and flutter
behind the wall

"Juditka, it's a wonderful thing, these recordings. It is only that … you will never understand." A look caresses my face, slides off. My hand seems to hold an object. My questions seem to touch their lives. It's an illusion. Two films superimposed on each other. Their lives. My hand.

"Tell me what it was like in your village. Tell me what you did when you got up, what the school looked like, the house and the woods, tell about your parents, brothers, sisters, uncles and aunts, tell me everything!" "In our village…" Hari begins, then stops, smiling. "But my dear, I have already told you everything…" I had long since recorded everything he remembered and was willing to tell, but I wanted to be with him. After *Shachris*, we walked the streets aimlessly. We began to feel cold and entered a café. On Shabes it is forbidden to touch money. I wanted to invite him, but he would not hear of it. "My sweetheart, it's out of the question."

"In my village, some seventy years ago, there was nothing, absolutely nothing. Behind our house were the mountains, with bears and wolves, and in front of it, the road and the railway—the main tourist attraction. There were woods, only woods … the endless, impenetrable forest." He leans back into his chair and looks at me, waiting for the effect. Then suddenly, he begins to laugh.

Data. Splinters scattered on the ground. Our words: the lid. Underneath: the unspeakable. I tried to resolve the contradictions. Now I leave them alone—let them be. They feel all right cuddled up in the warmth. The contradictions are the home we have to dwell in.

The task was to not run away. Not hide behind the façade of intelligent explanations. Their secret is impossible to solve. Their secret we live—our life.

Do you want to collect objects, or rather to see your own face in the disintegration of lives?

Why did I not search for my grandfather? "He did not come back…" my mother said. Where did it happen? On the road? In a camp? Nobody from his group survived—there are no eyewitnesses. Perhaps one day their souls will emerge on the other side of the earth; they will spring up and bloom. Let the wings of their story spread and shelter those holding the Book of Silence.

My "informants"! White silence grew around and within them. When their bodies fell into bed after a long day's work, their minds, against their will, set out on the journey of remembrance. The broken plates of lives slipped and pressed against each other. The picture in front of their eyes blurred, until one night, sleeping pills were swallowed in the hope of escaping from the lies—into the land of truth.

After decades of silence, the world suddenly became curious to know how so many people disappeared in such a short time. They were called upon to testify about what was done to them. But it is as if no one would be interested in their *lives*—the life they lived when they lived it. And if you only ask how it ended, then … It is like the rows of darkened windows in the night: the innocently sleeping white pretenses and lies do not hear that, on the abandoned square, someone screams the scream of the untold miracles—the *once really were lives*.

During the seventies, our meetings were like a secret memorial service. They were not ready to talk. It was enough to record melodies. These recordings were the atonement—theirs and mine—for our unforgivable sin: being alive.

In the nineties, they began to speak. Trembling, with shivers running down my spine, I resolved to tape *those stories*—the stories I should have never heard.

"Dayenu."

It was the sense of wonder on his face when he prayed that had made me want to record Zelmanovics. I got to know him in the nineties, at the time when, after almost a decade of absence, I began to visit Budapest again. By then I had analyzed dozens of hours of *nusach* and *davenen*. Still, I could not resist approaching him; something in his melodies compelled me. He prayed with an expression of incredulity, reminiscent of a small child who stares at the world, unable to comprehend how the grownups can take it seriously.

As agreed, I visited him on a Sunday. I rang the bell and heard the quickening of footsteps. Our glances met for a second; then he looked down, as if embarrassed, and, after murmuring a quick greeting, he led me inside. I was surprised to see his wife in the living room where we were supposed to have our session. I greeted her and prepared myself for a short, polite conversation. But she did not seem intent on leaving. "Why don't you take out the tape recorder?" she asked. I set up the equipment. "Why don't you start the tape?" I started the tape. "You came here to record songs," she began. "But it's not songs you should record. It's this." And she began to tell a story.

I stared at the trembling red needle of the volume window. I closed my ears … I shut off my brain ... the whole time … for all the days of my life … for as long as the stories last.

When, on a visit to Hungary the following summer, I called Zelmanovics, his wife informed me of his death. By then, her stories of apocalypse were catalogued without me having listened to them or even checked whether there was anything on the tape.

Our remaining meetings that summer were gentle and uneventful. My recording sessions are like a film forever on repeating: Zelmanovics sings, his body swaying back and forth, his eyes fixed on the letters. I sit opposite him, my eyes moving between the words of the prayer, the tape recorder and his face. We record a prayer and discuss the next piece. We record another prayer and talk some more. We take a break, eat a few butter cookies and discuss the political situation and the inflation. Every now and then, he tells me stories "from before."

When Zelmanovics *davened*, it was impossible to tell whether he was weeping, laughing, speaking or singing. His *davenen* was all of these together: it was prayer. Prayer meant life and life meant the apocalypse and everything that it had swept away. The horrors and joys of the past were like a kaleidoscope of colorful, broken glass.

During our recording of the *Haggadah*, we come to the *dayenu*. This poem recounts the story of the exodus in a sequence of verses, each of which follows the same pattern: Had God only done … even that would have been "*dayenu,*" that is, sufficient for us. In today's communities, the word *dayenu* is almost universally sung to a loud, optimistic and dance-like melody.

"This?" Zelmanovics turns to me with his usual bewildered look. "We had no song for this. We just read it. But if you insist ... all right, I'll recite it for you..." His *dayenu* consists of four notes—the same melodic motive repeated over and over. You cannot tell whether this text, a declaration of acceptance of God's ways, evokes pride, anger or sorrow in him. The simplicity of his recitation is like a vessel that holds whatever you wish to hear. Zelmanovics looks at me, and, seeing that I have understood, closes the book. "*Ennyi volna...*"—"That's all."

But perhaps it is a question: "*Dayenu?*" "Is that all?" "Is it possible ... this life and this history ... is this enough for one to carry on with faith?"

"When did you tell your children? I mean, what happened..." I do not know what made me ask this question.

"I don't think I ever told them. They knew it. They knew the essence. And the details transpired ... somehow ... gradually," he answers.

"It was the same for me. My parents did not speak about these things. But somehow I knew."

"What is there to tell? That before being shot into the Danube, they were asked to take off their shoes so that they wouldn't go to waste? When my grandchildren were small, I took them to the Danube; it's a ten-minute walk from here. The memorial with the shoes did not exist then. I let them play near the water, while I watched the reflections of the railings and the ropes of the ships. But sometimes, they did not play. They sat there next to me, looking at the waves. Children understand... What do your parents do?"

"They are doctors."

"They must have been very young. It's easier to go on with your life when you are young."

"When you *daven*, there is always ... I don't know how to say it ... a sense of memory. As if *davenen* were really ... for *them*."

"Perhaps... Well, as a matter of fact, I have always *davened* this way. That is the tradition. That is how we did it before the war, already as children. Back then, things were different—the *davenen* and also the songs. There was a different atmosphere."

"Atmosphere...?"

"It's hard for me to talk about this. It's not that we were mourning all the time. On the contrary, we laughed a lot—even in poverty! Basically, we were optimistic. But there was something in the air … and you could feel especially in the prayer that there was something in the air … a bit of … I don't know … a feeling that things were not stable and you could never know what was about to come, and that we do not quite understand … this whole thing that surrounds us. And so everything had a touch of…"

"Sadness…" I say almost involuntarily.

"Yes, sadness, perhaps that is the word. No, actually, I am not sure. Well, we can talk about this the next time you come. When are you leaving?"

"Wednesday."

"That means you cannot come again."

"No, unfortunately."

"Well then, we'll see each other next year. Will you call me when you come back next summer?"

"Of course."

As usual, what I should have said occurred to me when I was already outside. It is not sadness. It is rather hesitation. Hesitation, stumbling, drifting, glancing, gazing, wondering… A tentative and timid question that hovers in the air, over the prayer and above all things: "Is it really…?" And an answer: "… that would be it, that's all…" Which is, in reality, a question.

Today, the Orthodox synagogue at Kazinczy Street is a tourist site. The women's galleries are closed to visitors but—after buying their tickets—tourists are welcome to walk around in the men's section on the ground floor. I tip the guard to open the gate to the stairway that leads up to the galleries. "Just for you … don't tell anyone. It is forbidden to allow tourists upstairs because we don't have enough personnel to watch them," he informs me. "Have a quick look; do it fast. But don't go to the third floor—that's supposed to be locked anyway. Nobody has been up there since the war except for the workers who fixed the place, because … you should know that this is a valuable building. It's a national monument and architectural rarity. It was in terrible condition; the benches were broken and there was plaster falling from the ceiling. It was dangerous.

Now they painted the walls, torn out the benches and threw them into a pile. Nobody needs them anyway."

Twenty or so years ago, during the High Holidays, it was here, in the third-floor gallery, where I sat alone during the services. I arrived in the morning when it was still dark, and left in the evening when it was dark again.

I had climbed the stairs toward loneliness, toward them, into myself—an escape into thousand year old, thrown out melodies—a finely tuned asylum of words. My secret: the name on the bench—the name of someone who did not come back. *For whom* was I hiding?

I am voiceless. The half-formed reality of time around me—colors and sounds of time long gone, gold and blue glimmer behind grey walls, footsteps on chunks of plaster of painted flowers, dust on my fingers as I wipe clean the golden nameplate, and from the distance: the snow-covered greyness of prayers. I recall the fear. Whose fear? Whose sounds?

I doze in the cloud of their prayer; I dream in the bright-blue radiance of their belief. Their prayer: a cloud bleeding from swelling whiteness, depression under the dark dome of a winter sky stripped of time. Their prayer: the glimmer of gold and blue, the bright sky of the untold story of the name, and in the evening, when the last light carves itself into the darkness behind the columns and the candles, the brilliance of the turquoise sky squeezes your heart.

Whose turquoise? Whose darkness?

Our worlds collide. A question mark hovers over the page where you have written these words: they, I, we, together.

New World

Since I had left Hungary illegally, I could not return for a long time. Two months after my first trip to Budapest, in 1989, the Communist regime collapsed. I looked in vain for my old friends from the synagogues. They had died or were nowhere to be found. At first, the realization of loss and the absurd idea that I would have to "replace" them with new prayer leaders paralyzed me. I realized that from now on, I would be working with even older people and thus be constantly dealing with death. I would make plans and calculate the number of years—theirs and mine.

I found wonderful prayer leaders—Erbst (Hari), Fóti, Goitein, Mrs. Oberländer, Zelmanovics and others—but no community where I could have lived through the mystery of the ritual as I remembered it. The opening of the borders made it possible for American and Israeli Orthodox organizations to help reshape Jewish religious life in Hungary. Within less than a decade after the fall of Communism, the traditional communities disappeared. They were replaced by communities of the young, the healthy and the energetic, by a religion in the present tense that was transparent, obvious and immediate. The service became an attainable reality, and precisely for this reason, it seemed utterly unreal to me.

In the milieu from which I came, the things of the world drifted through the ambiguous gravitational fields of past and future. The present was constantly evolving, but its evolution lacked direction. When I listened to the concerts of Annie Fischer or József Réti at the Academy of Music, it was like witnessing an event that had taken place at the beginning of the twentieth century. The transformation of the tangible aspects of life seemed irrelevant. The ambience of times long gone remained in the air, a sensation impossible to describe in words. I felt the same way in the synagogues, where the smell of the past never cleared.

After the war, Jewish life in Hungary—as everywhere in Europe, if it survived at all—was shattered. Communities were dispersed, buildings ruined and religious practice disrupted. During the Communist period, it was impossible to keep even the most basic religious rules. Wherever one looked, one saw corrosion and decay.

Yet it seemed that for those who kept it, the soul of the Jewish religion had remained intact, even though anxiety and fear were palpable everywhere. The ways of religious life emerged gradually, a texture woven from memories, dreams, desires and possibilities—whatever was remembered and possible in those circumstances. The services were haphazard, and there was always a bit of hesitancy in the air. As though the prayers were unaware of their power, they stumbled in search of an ideal. This ideal was simultaneously clear and ambiguous: it was a *sense* of the essence of the religion, a global attitude toward life. Around this amorphous feeling lingered a collage of little details—fragments of religious practices retrieved from memory, gleaned from the sacred books or learned from each other.

"It must have been different before the war, more solid, precise and unified," I used to provoke them. But the answer was always something like this: "Of course, it was different. But back then there was also a lot of confusion. It was never simple. Do you believe that before the war, we never asked how far one should push the old ways of religious life—and if not those ways, then what and how? Do you think we didn't love the sound of the organ and the sweet choirs of the modern services, which we sometimes secretly listened to, although at the same time we despised and detested them? Or that assimilation wasn't a big question mark for us, or that the idea to leave tradition and religion behind never crossed our minds? That's how it is with tradition: one would like to be at both places at the same time. It's the same today and in every era: people would like to be traditional but also modern. And nobody knows how…"

But the leaders of the new religious communities sent from Israel and the United States knew how. I remember when, in the early phase of the new era during in the 1990s, I went to the kosher restaurant Hanna's in the Kazinczy Street synagogue complex. Like in Communist times, the most diverse people gathered there: a haphazard assemblage of lonely souls—people with no opportunity to honor the eve of Shabes with a ritual family dinner. As if I had never left, I found a group of people I knew and sat down with them, among some elderly men and women who accepted me almost like a member of the family.

The Americans sat separately. One could spot them immediately; they wore shiny black outfits, spoke in sharp voices and everything about them was decisive and energetic. When they finished eating, some of the men walked around, sat for a moment with the locals, listened to their complaints, and promised to send the "poor folks" this or that upon returning to their land of abundance.

After the brief exchange of complaints and promises, the circling missionaries returned to their table with stacks of little books containing the texts of *bentshn* and *zmires*—the blessing after the meal and the poems for the first meal of Shabes. "Here it comes," the old man sitting next to me whispered in my ear, "just wait, in a minute we'll be bulldozed over…" The little books were distributed at the American table, opened—and it began. They sang the *zmires*, one after the other, without skipping a single verse, let alone an entire song; they sang the texts busily and diligently and with great confidence in the order in which they appeared in the book.

The moment they began to sing, conversation ceased. From then on, you heard nothing but their razor-sharp, shrieking melodies. Our people did not join in; they felt embarrassed. As if they had been left standing on the platform of a backward village, watching the train make its way across rich lands.

I often ask myself why I feel so uncomfortable during the *zmires* sessions of modern Orthodox Jews, and why I felt relaxed hearing those old men in Budapest in the seventies, even though the sloppiness of their singing puzzled me. Perhaps it is because I like to see things disintegrate. More precisely: I like to see the frame of things disintegrating. If the frame is too attractive, the essence becomes lost. It is difficult for me to cope with situations that show no sign of doubt or hesitation—nothing that makes you wonder or ask questions. I am unable to take seriously anything that projects cloudless optimism, unshaken belief, or confident know-how without so much as a hint of self-irony. Those young men around their Shabbat table did not realize how close the forced happiness of their *zmires* came to my experiences of Communist singing contests.

At the shabby Shabes dinners and *shalashides* gatherings of the seventies, I did not feel people were trying to prove anything. We were enjoying an idle hour at the end of Shabes, with all the haphazard feelings and atmospheres that this hour could contain— even sleepiness or boredom. Their songs were of people who lived by faith—but this faith was full of questions. Their songs were of those who knew that perfection in faith was impossible, that life is but a desperate attempt to hold the air, and that the world is on the brink of collapse. They evoked the world as it really is—then and now, always and everywhere.

The historic change suddenly made me into one of the "old timers." I found myself speaking of the "old days," meaning Jewish life in Budapest before 1989. Indeed, from the perspective of developments taking place in the nineties, and even more in the years after the millennium, the religious practice of the seventies seemed like an unbroken continuation of the tradition from "back then," from before the war. This practice disintegrated before my eyes, and within a few years faded out of existence.

In spite of the feeling of loss, the nineties were a period of relief and optimism. People told me: "Every day, I see something disappearing. Those things that until now were natural for us… One day you wake up and look around and it is nowhere to be found and there isn't even anyone who remembers. Even the best, the most precious things are forgotten. It is only now that I know with certainty that Jewish life as we knew it is gone forever. But after all, is it really so important? … That was our life and this is something else. Perhaps that's how it should be … with lives … let it go."

"Yes," I keep reminding myself, "that's how it should be; let it go."

Grunewald

When I began this research, I hoped that one day I would see the divergent lines meet; that once I had distanced myself from it I would see a coherent traditional life, with an essence and a sense of direction. I was searching fanatically and single-mindedly for the cohesive force—the secret of the *silence behind* their melodies. Years passed. That generation died out—and with it its beliefs, anxieties and hesitations. The questions I asked those days are left floating in the air—unresolved and unaccounted for.

Each new scholarly discovery and each new personal experience drives me further from what I set out to do twenty or so years ago: to write a *coherent* book about the music of prayer as the expression of the life and culture of the Jews in Eastern Europe. How can Hari's prayer be defined as culture if we accept that culture is "a complex whole which includes knowledge, belief, art, morals, law, custom and any other capabilities and habits acquired by man as a member of society"? His context is a collage of heterogeneous realities, stretching from impoverished and backward village life, deportation, professional occupation in an urban Communist milieu, a modern Central European cultural environment with theater and music, and a variety of Jewish traditions, ranging from rigidly Orthodox to Hassidic and liberal.

Why do we understand each other so well? Is it because he reminds me a bit of my step-grandfather? Or because we attended—and enjoyed—the same concerts in the 1970s, when we did not yet knew each other? Or because we agree that about the deportations and the concentration camps one should only speak in a delicate and silent voice?

I am sifting through my notes from my years at the Academy of Music and find a scrap of paper with my undeveloped, irregular handwriting: "The most important thing: the barely audible voices from behind the wall." Was this sentence provoked by the sound of the prayer house? Or is this the afterthought of my parents' heated conversation in subdued voices coming from their room? Or did I write this after a concert of Annie Fischer for which I could not get a ticket and heard it from outside the hall, or after my long wait backstage at Charles' school ready to join the orchestra in the next piece? I find recurring *faces*, overlapping relations and situations, momentarily shared experiences and sentences.

I shuddered when I heard Hari say, "Outsiders do not understand this, so it's better to keep it to ourselves." This sentence, which resonates like warning bells from my early memories, forms a bond between us in our world of silence. I heard this sentence not only at home, but also from my teacher, György Kroó, chairman at the Department of Musicology and director of the Music Division of the Hungarian Radio, the "Gyuri" of Hari's story who exchanged concert tickets for *tsibere*. Similarly to "Gyuri," Hari, my parents and grandparents, I was forced all too often to keep things to myself during my youth in Hungary, as well as later, in France, America and Israel, and leave the field of conversation before anything could really be said.

Is there, has there ever been, can there ever be a life with a coherent and consistent worldview? If there is such a thing, I must have missed it. We all missed it: my parents and grandparents, my teachers and friends, and the prayer leaders I came to know. And after the millennium, we really let it go. Today, it is enough for us to discover a sudden connection that for a moment makes sense of the collage we call life. Rupture is healed by empathy—for a moment, before our lives disintegrate back into chaos, we look into each other's eyes and see.

Unlike most scholars, I do not think of Jewish prayer melodies as coherent structures in which every element has its proper function and the connections are logical and transparent. Perhaps no music could be fit into one coherent and total structure, but traditional *davenen* and *nusach* certainly do not. What I see is a continuous flow of overlapping structures in a field of intensities in which lines of connection emerge, constantly cohering or falling apart, strengthening or annulling each other. Melodies travel their unending journey of transformation, and at any given moment the sound is complex, confused and seemingly arbitrary, like a snapshot. It is like looking at a landscape through the holes of a torn cloth, seeing scattered and incomprehensible fragments of connecting and disconnecting multitudes.

"It happens after I've been working for a while, maybe a few weeks, on one small motive, a few sounds, repeating them over and over until I do not even think about them anymore—they just happen to be there, like old friends. I start something else, a different piece with different sounds—the same thing. Suddenly, it hits me: the notes from the two pieces are actually the same. It is me, it is the instrument, it is this crazy idea of repeating notes that brings things together, things that were never meant to connect. But they do connect—in such a direct, such a natural, spontaneous way, as if they had been waiting all along for this to happen. Suddenly, the sounds are free, and everything flows together like a big ocean…"

(Ben Niran on composing on and practicing the marimba)

I am writing this book in Grunewald, an elegant suburb of Berlin, on the top floor of a bizarre, pseudo-Renaissance fortress bedecked with mosaics depicting mythological scenes and Latin quotations, a product of the architectural fantasies of some lonely, megalomaniac Russian millionaire. My thoughts wander between the Dorian columns of the balcony and the dense forest beyond, against which the curved patterns of the stucco roof stand out like Christmas ornaments. My mind melts in this lush richness and my voice lies buried in my throat.

What am I doing here?

I am waiting for the winter and the sour odor of poverty it brings. Snow swells on the cotton grey horizon and rivers of dark red water seep from hollow cavities. The forest's myriad lianas grow into a confused map of entangled paths; the brownish red tapestry is sliced by thousands of shimmering, snow-covered branches—like crystal ornaments pressed into a bleeding surface. The grey clouds turn inside out to expose a yellow river, and the silence of a deafening cry reverberates in my ear.

How did prayer sound in a barely heated room in a faraway village, surrounded by the magic colors of the winter morning?

Day after day, I stare out the window. My mind knows in all certainty that the mirage of the winter forest resonates in the sound of the Jewish prayer house. I feel as if I were standing, terrified and confused, in the last row of that secret prayer house many years ago. The brown and grey of the men's clothes form disorganized patches of color. They sway back and forth rhythmically, like branches in the wind—each in his own tempo. They emit tiny, hurried smoke-rings of melody through their constantly moving lips. Silent cries fly across the cloud of prayer. Here and there, an outcry—the arrow of a "vey" or an "oy," a scream or a sob—carves its way through the surface of sound, following an unwritten rule. The melodies—lives scattered and secrets whispered—collide and mingle like the entangled branches of a forest. I don't see the trees—only the flow of colors. I don't hear voices—only sound. I don't know when it began—it has always been.

In Berlin, I am silent. Voiceless stranger, shadow of shadows, shattered half-existence incapable of defending itself, sound that resists remembering while knowing everything, an outcry ashamed of its own voice, light shamed by its vibration. I walk through smoke and mist, frosted glass and negative images—shards on the glass membrane of my eyes... I write. I write every day; I write and write.

My quiet walks in the city are the memorial; my rushing words in distress, the prayer. Why them, why that fate, why those prayers? Why here, why me, why now? I pretend to be looking for the answer, as if I did not know. We never reach the place we set out for. We are at home where we never wanted to be.

Tulips

I should make order. I should do my research. Dig up the real names of my informants, which they often did not tell me; find out their Hebrew names, their dates of birth and death according to the Jewish calendar. Say *Kaddish* for them and light the candles. The names. There used to be a man in a brown jacket in one of the prayer houses. I have never heard singing more perfect and inspired, a voice so beautiful and pure. I was too shy to tell him this; I did not even dare to ask his name. I must find him, or at least somebody who knew him. I must find them, those whom I lost—their friends and wives, relatives and acquaintances.

I begin with Ilonka Goitein. I sit on the couch at my place where I used to be sitting while recording her husband when he was still alive. My terrible mistake suddenly dawns on me. Why did I not talk to Ilonka before? Where are they—the women? Besides Aunt Éva, I worked only with men. It is true that in the traditional service, the *baltfile* must be man. Still, the women have a strong presence and a unique viewpoint.

During the conversation, the inevitable question comes up:

"How did you survive?"

She stares at me, surprised.

"Didn't you know? I'm not Jewish… So you're wondering how it is that I, a non-Jew, know about *kashrut*? It's simple."

"We fell in love in the sixties. Once I was invited for dinner and when I wanted to help, his mother would not let me into the kitchen—she stood in front of the kitchen entrance and stretched her arms, blocking the way. When this happened for the third time, I took him aside: 'Stop playing games with me. I know you are Jewish and keep kosher.' He turned pale. I was just a simple administrator and he was the executive director of a huge, immensely successful company with branches all over the country and with business with the West. But those were Communist times and the Jews had to remain invisible."

"He couldn't fool me. I come from a small town. There were many Jews there. Our neighbors were Jewish and my best friends were Jewish girls, so of course I knew what *kashrut* was. I also knew the holidays. I saw it around me all the time; some holidays took place practically in our backyard. Believe me, it's not a big deal, *kashrut* and the difference between Jews and Christians; at least in our town, this was not a problem."

"He loved my pastries. He used to say to our guests that, in his opinion, though he might be biased, I bake the best kosher pastries in town. He often went on business trips to the Soviet Union; this was a privilege in those days. Whenever he was invited to a business dinner, he would say he had an upset stomach and could only eat bread. He lived on bread and yoghurt."

"The moment he reached the airport, he would write me a postcard and mail it before he boarded the plane. It was always the same picture, the only card you could buy at the airport in those days: a Malév plane flying through the bright blue sky. Look, I have one here on the desk. It was love … it was true love between us."

"He was already a prayer leader many years before you began to record him. But I never went with him to the synagogue, not even after I converted. I was never the Churchgoing type, and that did not change with my new religion."

"I light the candles every Shabes and holiday. I light candles on his *yahrzeit*, and on the *yahrzeit* of his father and mother and brothers and sisters. I buy the Jewish calendar at the beginning of the year and mark the dates. I am sure he would be happy if he knew. Who would light the candles if not me? I am the only one left from his family."

"Over the years, this apartment has become my home. I love the large rooms, the broad windows and the high ceiling. My sisters say that it's badly constructed and noisy. 'What noise?' I ask. You see, I am so used to the noise that I don't even hear it any more. I am used to these Jewish books, to the candles and holidays, to everything that belonged to him and to our life together."

"If I win the lottery, I will have an elevator built for this house. I have had such a good life here! Communism or not—I have nothing to complain about. The only thing missing is an elevator. In a few years, I won't be able to climb the stairs to the top floor. I am thinking of going to an old age home; there is one not far from here. They would take care of the apartment and everything in it, except those things you want to keep or give away yourself. But there isn't much space in the little rooms they offer, so most of the things will have to go. My sisters say I should sell this apartment and buy one with an elevator. But I cannot imagine emptying these shelves and cupboards, touching each object, sorting and throwing them out piece by piece. I simply could not do it. I will throw a big party, invite my family and everyone who knew him and let them take whatever they want—and then leave. What do you think? Should I do it?"

There can be no visit to Budapest without me seeing Hari. It is a pity that the lilacs are not yet in bloom, because he would have given me a bucketful like he did last year.

"Did you know that the water level in the Danube will reach a peak today?" he asks while arranging the pillows on the couch.

"The lower bank is completely flooded. It looks as if Pest and Buda are being pushed apart," I inform him.

"They say it's like a fair. People come from all over the country to see the flood, and some clever types have set up stands on the bank selling this and that. It's too bad I don't feel well these days and cannot go," he complains.

"The shoes are under water. The Holocaust monument, you know," I say.

"The shoes are under water," he repeats, then suddenly falls silent, as if something had just occurred to him. We sit for some time without saying a word. Then he breaks the silence.

"Will you film the flood?"

"Of course. I have my camera with me. I'm going straight there."

"I hope you don't want to film me. You're laughing, and that's not a good sign. I know you, my dear; you are capable of anything. But we agreed, remember…?"

"I just came to see you."

It was not the conversation or the laughter, the blue sky or the fact that we understood each other without words that broke my heart, while at the same time filling it with sweetness. It was the way he curled up in the armchair like a child, as if he had never known nights overflowed by death. As if he had always believed in the protection of words, as if he could remain like this for the rest of his life—*between gold and forgetting*.

I meet Bence at Café Europa. We have not seen each other for thirty years. We speak the same language, we grew up in the same little village: the Jewish circles of Communist Budapest. With him, there is nothing to explain and nothing to be ashamed of. I know where he failed and he knows where I failed. It feels good to justify your way of life to someone who does not need your excuses.

"Actually, I did not mean to become religious," he launches his defense. "I only wanted to learn. It annoyed me that they knew things I did not have the slightest idea about. I was an incorrigible intellectual; I could not accept that someone would know a subject, especially languages and texts, better than I did. I began by learning the prayers, Hebrew and Aramaic, then came the customs, the Torah and the commentaries, and there was no stopping it."

"For my part, I did not want to sink too deep into it. It was just as well not to understand everything exactly but remain a bit ignorant, at the periphery—always somewhat a stranger. I did not want to be lured into religion," I say, presenting my excuse.

"It's all because of Moshe Weiss at Kazinczy Street," he continues. "He was special—an amazing scholar and a unique personality. He was passionate but never rigid. Everything he thought came from within. Whenever he did something, he knew why he was doing it, he believed in it, and did it with faith, sincerely, and giving it his best. He accepted me as his disciple. I have never had a teacher like him."

"I will never forget those Yom Kippurs. The *musaf* and the *nile*! How he sang! It was like a cry torn from his heart."

"Oh, those Yom Kippurs! The *nile*!" Bence sighs. We remain silent for a while, immersed in our memories like an elderly couple.

"I did not dare go near him. He knew so much and was so inspired … so spiritual. He would not have even looked at me," I continue.

"That was a big mistake. He would have helped you. You were serious, you did this work with passion and were devoted to it and he always noticed these things. He would have even sung for you. Yes, I am certain that he would have sung the *nusach* for you, if only you'd have asked."

I like to create beautiful spaces around myself. Flowers are a small luxury I cannot do without. When spring comes, I buy red and yellow tulips. I push the vase to the edge of my desk in order to make space for the computer. It is a memorial, this pushing of the vase. Every gesture is a memorial.

I wave goodbye to my parents and proceed to passport control. I go through the glass door and look back, but I cannot see them anymore. I imagine them driving home on the poorly lit highway. My father drives, his bald head bobbing gently at every bump in the road. My mother turns toward him and strokes his head: "Aren't you tired?" "No, not at all," my father replies. I find the gate, sit down and open my cellphone. I hold it in my hand. We agreed that they would call when they got home.

As my years fly forward, the past deepens. I am weighed down by the memory of un-asked questions and the thought that my hesitations may have spoiled everything. I had been too shy to say what I felt, too shy to give. Unspoken phrases echo in my brain and in the sound of my blood my silences reverberate. This is my prayer that forever sings itself from within. I thank them and offer what I have.

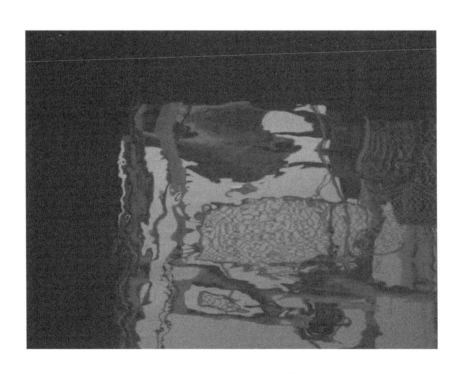

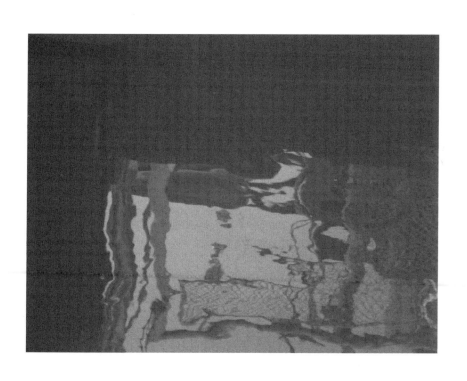

Transliteration

The spelling of Hebrew words in this book reflects mainly two dialects. The first dialect is the official standard pronunciation that shows the influence of the pronunciation patterns of German. This was taught in major schools like the Rabbinical Seminary in Budapest, and it was used, typically, by literate urban Jews, especially in the Western territories of Hungary. The second dialect shows affinity with the pronunciation patterns of Yiddish. It was used, in a variety of forms, in villages and towns alike in the Eastern and Northeastern regions of Hungary, and in the villages and among the more religious (usually Yiddish-speaking) communities in all parts of Hungary. This Hebrew dialect was the norm for most of the European Jews in the territories East of Hungary. Both dialects belong to what is normally called Ashkenazic, which differs from how Hebrew is spoken in present-day Israel.

In the spelling of Hebrew and Yiddish words, I tried to follow the sound of the word as it was pronounced. Therefore, in the text, Hebrew words are not transliterations of written letters. The spelling does not reflect those letters that were not pronounced, like א and ע, or the letter ה at the end of words. There is one exception: when the sound "y" (like in "yes") occurs as part of a diphthong for a vowel, I use "i" (oi, ai), but when it is the pronunciation of the consonant "י" (yod), I use "y." In one instance, there was no model in my ear or on the tape for the pronunciation of Hebrew, and this is the reading of *Akdomus*. Here, the transliteration is faithful to the written letters as much as possible, and the pronunciation reflects the situation in the story: the way I would have read the text at the time.

Each person in this book pronounces Hebrew according to his or her dialect. The pronunciation of the consonants is more or less the same; differences occur mostly in vowels and in the accentuation and the inner rhythm of the word as a whole. The variants are sometimes considerable, at other times minor, and several of them were impossible to reflect. This was the case, for instance, with "i" and "ü" in words like *shvies/shvües* or *borich/borüch*. The sound "i" in these words has numerous transitional shades between "i" and "ü" (but it is never entirely identical with the "ü" sound of the German language). For the sake of convenience, I used "i" for all variants. Somewhat similar is the situation with "o" and "u," where the pronunciation is often somewhere in between how these letters would sound in English (like the "o/u" in *adoinoy/adainoy*).

These nuances in pronunciation were considered to be extremely important by the people who appear in this book. It was of great consequence whether, for instance, one would use "u" or "i" or something between "i" and "ü" in the word *boruch/borich/borüch*, whether one said *mincha* or *minche*, *kashrut* or *kashrus*, *musaf* or *misef*, *kiddush* or *kidish*, *Simchas tauro* or *Simches taire*. Pronunciation was associated with background, provenance, and education, and was considered an indicator of the religiousness of a person. Neolog Jews went to the synagogue, but those who were serious about the religion went to *shul*. The way one pronounced the names of the holidays שבועות and

סוכות amounted to a declaration of one's congregational alliance and social status. At the Rabbinical Seminary, and for upper class Jews, these were the holidays of *Shavuaus* and *Sukkaus*; for most people in this book they were *Shvies* and *Sikes*.

It would not do justice to the personages in this book to standardize their language according to the official version. For these people, it was out of the question to call the third ritual meal of the Shabes by its official Ashkenazic name, *sholaush seudaus* (let alone *seudo shlishit*, which would be the correct form). I have never heard anybody say: "I go for *sholaush seudaus*," simply because those who would have used the official pronunciation belonged to the more assimilated Jews, and did not celebrate this ritual at all. Only those who said *shalashides* celebrated it.

But there was one instance when the more assimilated Jews accepted the Yiddish dialect of Hebrew. Although the official Ashkenazic pronunciation of Shabbat (Sabbath) is *Shabbos*, *Shabes* had become normative even in many Neolog congregations, and the two were used interchangeably and often alternately (sometimes even within the same sentence). It should also be noted that after the fall of Communism, with the transformation of the community at the influence of the religious leaders coming from America and Israel, several of the Yiddish-sounding forms current in their usage had become standard also among the Hungarian Jews. For instance, in the 1970s, only the more religious called the synagogue "*shul*," but by the late 1990s, this was commonplace among the Neologs as well.

This situation was at the same time confusing and fascinating, but it always impressed me as something full of life. In the text, I tried to reflect my fascination and confusion. As I was struggling to achieve a limited number of forms for each word, I realized that it was impossible to settle for a system of spelling that conveyed the many colorful sounds and at the same time was entirely consistent. I apologize for the eventual inconsistencies.

Hebrew and Yiddish words that became standard in English are spelled accordingly (like Hassid, Torah, yahrzeit, kibbutz, yeshiva, kaddish, kohen, kosher, etc.) except when the pronunciation of the person is significantly different from the accepted English. For instance, I use both Yom kippur and *Yomkiper*, Torah and *Taire*, depending on the speaker and the context.

Sounds in foreign words should be pronounced as in English except for those listed below.

Special consonants:

The consonant	Should always be pronounced as in
ch	loch
g	gap
sh	should
ts	tzigane
	(but "tz" when a word with this spelling had been accepted in English and/or in names)
tsh	Tchaikovsky
	(occurs in one word only: *bentshn)*

Note: When by chance "sch" occurs in a text, it does not denote the German "sch" (which would be pronounced "sh"), but is two sounds "s" + "ch" (like in "Pischi li sharey tsedek").

Vowels
Note that the table below is approximate; several vowels have variants as noted above.

The vowel	Should always be pronounced as in
a	father
ai	pilot
e	men (variants with shades of "é" sound like in prey)
ei	prey
i	see (but often short)
o	Paul
oi	boy
u	good

Acknowledgements

I would like to express my infinite gratitude first and foremost to all those who appear in this book, whether with their real name or under a pseudonym. I feel what I wrote at some point in the book: it was not me who wrote this text, but they whose stories it recounts. I would like to thank the prayer leaders whose stories I was not able to tell, among them most importantly Zoltán Simon, Emerich Deutsch and Yichak Eshel. The conceptualization and writing of this text could not have been possible without the support of the Wissenschaftskolleg zu Berlin and Bar Ilan University. It is impossible to mention here all those who helped me in the more than thirty year long research that formed the basis for this book—among them foundations, teachers, colleagues, students, assistants, and my family—and those scholars, writers, poets and friends who read the manuscript and whose criticism, suggestions and encouragement helped me immensely in the realization of the final form. I owe special thanks to Ádám Csillag and his crew for noticing the visual potential of this book and shooting several hours of invaluable documentary material for a film in progress; the photos on pages 218 and 219 are from this film and were taken by cameraman Tibor Varjas. I thank Ádám Halmos and Bence Sárközy and the staff of the Libri publishing house for their beautiful work in publishing the Hungarian version of this book. I thank the staff of CEU Press: Krisztina Kós for her creativity and energy, Ilse Josepha Lazaroms for her sensitivity in editing the text, and Károly Pavela for his patience and effectiveness in helping with the design of this edition. I cannot thank Walter Zev Feldman enough for his continual encouragement, and for his devotion through long nights reading and re-reading the final versions. I owe a debt of gratitude to Katalin Kátai, who supported me from the moment she first read the manuscript and helped me ever since in every way. Finally, I thank my son, Ben Niran; I would not have been able to create this book without his stimulating ideas and inspiring personality.